DATE DUE

OVERTURNING WRONGFUL CONVICTIONS

SCIENCE SERVING JUSTICE

ELIZABETH A. MURRAY, PHD

Twenty-First Century Books / Minneapolis

Author Dedication: This book is dedicated to all individuals who have been falsely accused within the legal system, particularly those whose charges resulted in wrongful conviction and who may be currently serving an undeserved sentence. Great tribute is due to the members of exoneration organizations who devote their time to free the innocent. I also want to honor all police officers, attorneys, judges, jurors, and my fellow forensic scientists, whose good work leads to findings of truth and justice.

Twenty-First Century Books
A division of Lerner Publishing Group, Inc.
241 First Avenue North
Minneapolis, MN 55401 USA

For updated reading levels and more information, look up this title at www.lernerbooks.com.

Main body text set in Adobe Caslon Pro 11/15
Typeface proved by Adobe Systems

Library of Congress Cataloging-in-Publication Data

Murray, Elizabeth A.
    Overturning wrongful convictions : science serving justice / by Elizabeth A. Murray, PhD.
        pages   cm
    Includes bibliographical references and index.
    ISBN 978-1-4677-2513-2 (lib. bdg. : alk. paper)
    ISBN 978-1-4677-6307-3 (EB pdf)
    1. Crime analysis—United States—Juvenile literature. 2. Vindication—United States—Juvenile literature. I. Title.
HV7936.C88M87 2015
364—dc23   2014017225

Manufactured in the United States of America
1 – VI – 12/31/14

CONTENTS

"It is better that ten guilty persons escape, than one innocent suffer."

—Sir William Blackstone, English jurist, judge, and politician, 1765

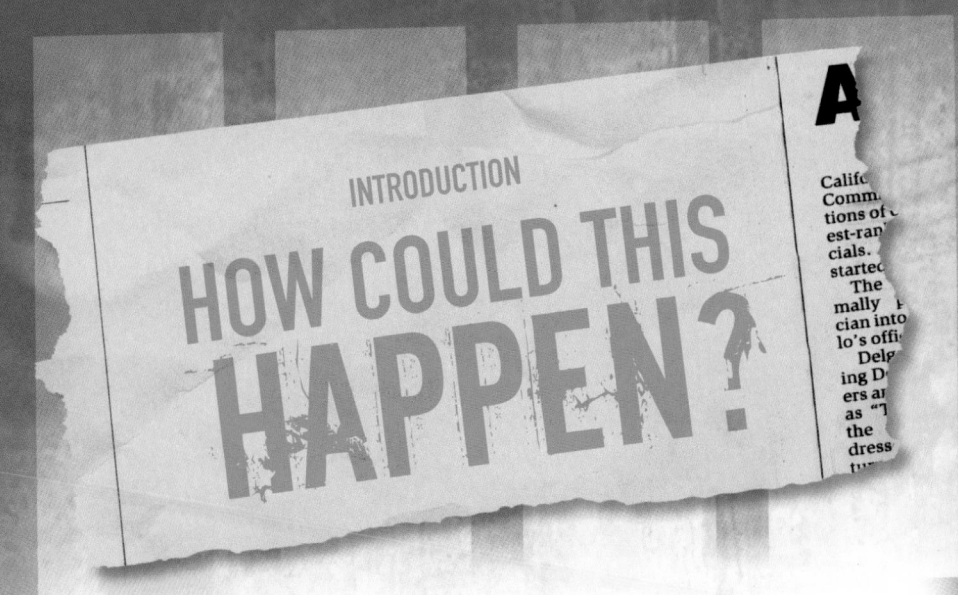

HOW COULD THIS HAPPEN?

On the night of April 19, 1989, members of a group of more than thirty teenagers stormed through New York City's Central Park committing robberies and assaults. One of the victims of attack was twenty-eight-year-old investment banker Trisha Meili, who was out jogging. Around 9:30 p.m., Meili was brutally raped, beaten, and left for dead in a clump of bushes at the edge of the woods. She had been tied up with her own shirt. More than four hours later, when police officers and paramedics arrived on the scene, they determined that Meili was in a coma due to massive blood loss. In addition, her skull had been fractured to the point that her left eye was hanging out of its socket. Twelve days later, Meili came out of her coma. She had survived the brutal attack but remembered nothing about it. Authorities promised to find those responsible for the vicious assault on this bright, successful young woman.

On the night of the attack itself, police had rounded up some of the more than thirty teenagers in Central Park. Of those teens, the police ultimately settled on five fourteen- to sixteen-year-old suspects as the assailants in Meili's attack. Some of the youths had a history of problems at school. Others came from broken homes, and one was hearing impaired and developmentally challenged. All were from Harlem, an impoverished neighborhood of New York with a large minority population. None of the five teens had ever been in trouble with the law before.

The situation was racially charged from the outset. Meili was white, four of the suspects were black, and one was Hispanic. Normal police guidelines in cases involving juveniles call for withholding the identity of underage suspects from the public at the outset of an investigation. This practice is also the law in many US states. Yet, in the Meili case, authorities released the names of the five teens. The media then published their photographs and addresses before police had formally arrested and charged them. The suspects, who became known as the Central Park Five, were Antron McCray, Kevin Richardson, Yusef Salaam, Raymond Santana, and Korey (sometimes spelled Khorey or Kharey) Wise.

During police questioning, authorities separated the boys. Throughout many hours of individual police interrogation, officers falsely told each teen that the others had blamed him. Four of the five suspects confessed on videotape to the attack, at the same

> **"I FELT LIKE THESE GUYS ARE REALLY ANGRY AND . . . THEY MIGHT TAKE US TO THE BACK OF THE PRECINCT AND KILL US."**
> —*Yusef Salaam, 2012*

time minimizing their own involvement. Yusef Salaam said of his questioning by police, "The tone was very, very scary. I felt like these guys are really angry and, you know what, they might take us to the back of the precinct and kill us." Salaam was the only one to refuse to sign a confession. All the same, officers wrote down an admission they assigned to him, and the other four teens pointed to him in their confessions. Within the next few weeks, however, all four teens changed their stories, saying they had made false admissions under extreme pressure from police.

WHAT DID THE EVIDENCE REVEAL?

Crime scene photos showed an 18-inch-wide (45.7 centimeter) trail of bloodstain and flattened grass between the lane where Meili had been knocked down and the bushes where she was discovered. The narrow trail did not suggest multiple attackers in a group effort to drag her into the brush. Investigators did not find the victim's blood on any of the suspects. Not a single witness to any events observed in the park that night could identify any of the five teens. The DNA profile from Meili's rape matched none of the young men. Although hairs found on one suspect were similar to the victim's hair, no physical evidence positively tied any of the teens to the crime.

Even so, all five juveniles were brought to trial and convicted in 1990. Among their various convictions for the attack on Meili were rape, assault, sexual abuse, and attempted murder. The confessions of guilt seemed to outweigh all other considerations. Each teen received the maximum sentence allowable based on age, ranging from five to fifteen years behind bars. Korey Wise, sixteen years old when the attack occurred, was tried as an adult and served the longest sentence. The names of each of the Central Park Five were also entered into New York's registry of criminal sex offenders.

When his punishment was announced, Kevin Richardson turned to his family and said, "Don't worry. The truth will come out. I'll never stop fighting. I never did this crime."

The guilty verdicts divided the nation. Some Americans celebrated the decision as a victory and praised police and prosecutors. Others were outraged, believing justice had not been served. Calvin O. Butts III, a local leader in Harlem stated, "The presumption of innocence was lost in the rush to judgment. People are not saying they forgive the crime. They're not saying they don't have compassion for that woman. All they're saying is, there is a considerable amount, an overwhelming amount, of reasonable doubt." C. Vernon Mason and William Kunstler, attorneys for Antron McCray and Yusef Salaam, claimed that the case had been built on racial prejudice and amounted to nothing more than a "legal lynching." Jurors later admitted that at least one of the defendants didn't have a good lawyer to argue his case.

THE EAST SIDE RAPIST

Twelve years later, in 2002, one of Wise's fellow prison inmates, Matias Reyes, approached him. After their conversation, Reyes requested to speak with authorities. Reyes confessed that, as a seventeen-year-old, he had been Meili's sole attacker. Known as the East Side Rapist for the part of New York in which he committed his crimes, Reyes was serving a long sentence. He had been convicted for five other rapes committed around the same period as the Central Park case and for the murder of a pregnant woman just two months after the attack on Meili. Authorities had not compared the DNA from Meili's case to the DNA from a rape that had occurred just two days earlier and in the same neighborhood. If they had, the testing would have quickly shown that Meili was also one of the victims of the East Side Rapist. Reyes's DNA had been sampled before he went to prison. However, authorities did not compare it to the DNA from Meili's attack until after he confessed.

Forensic testing showed that Reyes's DNA profile was a match to the semen found on Meili's sock. As a result of the DNA evidence, District Attorney Robert Morgenthau requested a hearing before the New York State Supreme Court in which he recommended the court vacate (reverse) the 1990 convictions of the Central Park Five and dismiss the criminal charges against the teens. All guilty verdicts against the five young men from 1990 were vacated in late 2002.

SERVING SOMEONE ELSE'S TIME

What makes up for the years of freedom the Central Park Five lost? What can erase the suffering of the men's families and the damage to their reputations? How can the harsh realities of prison life ever be forgotten? Santana has said about his fellow prisoners, "In the beginning it was very hard because they perceived me as . . . a rapist [who had] committed one of the most heinous crimes in New York State history. My faith was gone, and I didn't know what to do." Regarding the tension and violence of prison life, McCray said, "It's real hectic in there, people dying over cigarettes. It was real crazy." Wise was unable to attend his father's funeral or grieve along with his family. He said, "When I heard that my dad had passed, it was hurting."

In 2012 the documentary film *The Central Park Five* returned the case to public attention. About the film, Yusef Salaam said, "It wasn't a popular thing to be one of us . . . [but the documentary] really gave us our lives back." In the summer of 2014, twenty-five years after the attack on Trisha Meili, the Central Park Five agreed to settle their lawsuit against the City of New York for $40 million.

The men known as the Central Park Five at the New York premiere of the 2012 documentary **The Central Park Five**, a film about their experiences of wrongful conviction. **From left to right:** Antron McCray, Raymond Santana, Kevin Richardson, Yusef Salaam, and Korey Wise.

EXONERATION

In the decades between 1989—when the Central Park Five were first accused—and mid-2014, more than 1,400 convicted people in the United States have been cleared of guilty verdicts in a process known as exoneration. Many of these individuals were serving time after being convicted of serious crimes, such as rape and murder, that they did not commit. Each of these stories of unjust incarceration involves a tragic loss of dignity and liberty. Each story of exoneration involves righting a terrible injustice.

It is impossible to know how many innocent people are sitting in prison at this moment. Studies suggest that around 2 to 5 percent of all US inmates did not commit the crimes for which they were convicted. That translates to approximately 40,000 to 100,000 people currently unjustly behind bars in the United States alone. This statistic also means that the vast majority of people in prison do belong there.

The focus of most attempts to exonerate people who have been falsely convicted is on the worst offenses, such as murder and rape. These crimes carry the stiffest sentences, sometimes including the death penalty. For that reason, the majority of innocent people who have been convicted of less serious crimes will never be cleared.

"Anger is not a trait I was born with. It began in prison, and it grows each day. . . . For most of my life I took pride in being easygoing, slow to react, and naturally calm. But I have changed. . . . I wake up each morning to prison bars. . . . As soon as I open my eyes, I am mad. . . . I am so angry that complete madness cannot be far away."

—Calvin C. Johnson Jr., wrongfully convicted inmate (since exonerated), circa 1993

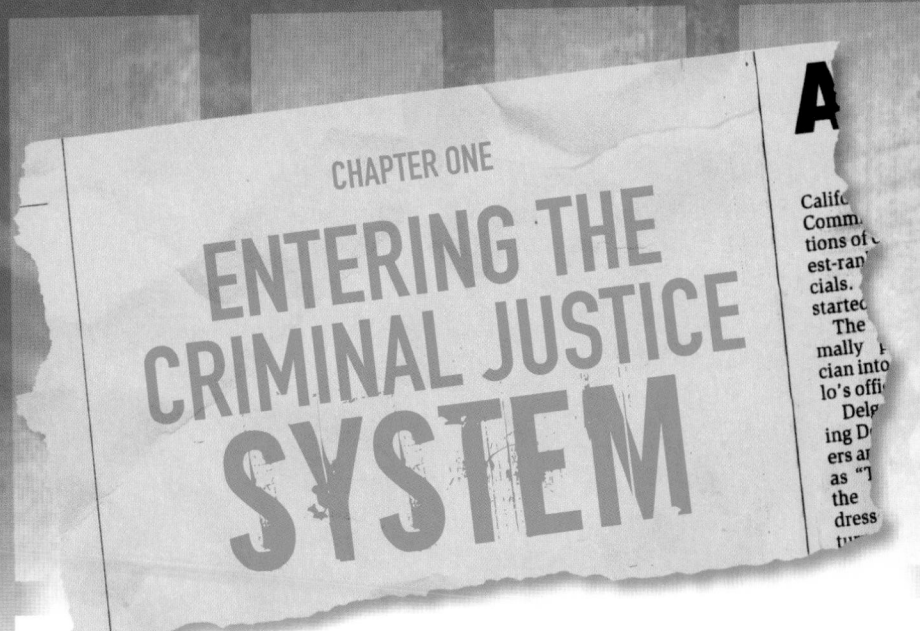

CHAPTER ONE

ENTERING THE CRIMINAL JUSTICE SYSTEM

Convictions and exonerations take place within the criminal portion of the US jurisprudence (legal) system. Criminal cases are those in which a person has broken a law. Civil cases involve disputes between people or institutions. Only in criminal cases do juries or judges decide guilt and innocence. The US legal system is based on the presumption that people are innocent in criminal matters until a judge or jury finds them guilty, based on evidence presented in the courtroom. In a criminal case, the responsibility to establish guilt—known as the burden of proof—lies with the government (local, state, or federal). Attorneys known as prosecutors represent the position of the government in these cases. The accused individual, known during the legal case as the defendant, is represented by one or more lawyers.

The location of a crime determines its jurisdiction, or the level of government with legal authority to prosecute the matter. This authority typically lies with a state. The county within the state where the crime took place undertakes the prosecution. If the crime occurs on federal property or the crime scene boundaries cross state lines, the federal government will prosecute the case. In some instances, jurisdictions will make agreements about which one will undertake the prosecution. In the United States, regardless of jurisdiction, the US Constitution protects the rights of individuals even before trial, such as during questioning or arrest by the police. The Constitution also specifies that any person charged with a crime is entitled to a speedy and fair trial. The guilt of that individual must be established beyond any reasonable doubt on the part of the judge or jury who hears the case.

ARREST AND CHARGES

An arrest by a police officer or a federal agent is the first step toward a criminal court case. Arrests can take place at the scene of a crime. They can also occur during questioning at police headquarters or after officers reach a logical conclusion that a person likely committed an offense. An arrest can also occur after a grand jury agrees, based on a review of information, that an arrest should be made. For example, following a murder, officers might seek and obtain legal permission to search a suspect's home. There, the police might find evidence such as blood on some of the suspect's clothing. Investigators would then present their findings to a judge or grand jury. If the judge or jury agrees that the evidence points strongly to the suspect's involvement in the killing, a warrant (legal authorization) would be issued for that person's arrest.

Officers can only make arrests if they have probable cause (strong suspicions they can later support before the court) to detain the suspect. A person cannot be arrested based only on mild suspicion. Probable cause is present when an officer witnesses an offense as it unfolds or if compelling circumstances lead the officer to believe a person broke the law. For example, a police officer might happen to observe a man with a duffel bag running from the scene of a bank robbery and thus consider him a likely suspect in the crime. If the officer is able to stop the man, the officer has the right to question him. (Police have the legal authority to question anyone, whether witness or suspect, at any time.) If, during questioning, the officer begins to believe the man is guilty of the robbery, or finds a large amount of cash in the duffel bag (which can be searched if the police have probable cause), the officer can make an arrest on the spot.

THE US CONSTITUTION PROTECTS THE RIGHTS OF INDIVIDUALS EVEN BEFORE TRIAL, SUCH AS DURING QUESTIONING OR ARREST BY THE POLICE.

The arrested person is then booked at a police station. There, officers take the suspect's fingerprints, obtain personal information (name, age, and physical features), and take a photographic mug shot. Police will also conduct a background check on the subject. Officers will collect and inventory any personal property with the suspect at the time, and the person will be placed in a holding cell.

Next, a court hearing takes place to formally announce the official charges against an accused individual. At that point, a judge or magistrate will decide, based on the crime and the arrested person's background, if the suspect will be held in jail.

RIGHTS AND RESPONSIBILITIES

Parts of the US Constitution's Bill of Rights protect individuals from unfair treatment in the legal process. Some of the provisions outline certain rights of people who find themselves in police custody in the United States. Other sections protect individuals from a police search of their body, vehicle, or home without a warrant, except in extreme emergencies where evidence may be destroyed or lives are at risk. (A pat-down procedure, during which police check for concealed weapons, is allowed.)

In the 1960s, the US Supreme Court established the Miranda warning. It not only protects citizens from unjust treatment but also ensures that information given legally to police may be used later in court. The police are required by law to read this warning out loud to an arrested suspect before interrogation. They must also do their best to ensure the person understands the warning. After an arrest, any information that comes from an interview in which the warning was not read cannot be used as evidence in court.

The Miranda warning is named for Ernesto Miranda (above). In 1966 the US Supreme Court ruled that Miranda's right to protect himself during police questioning had been violated. This decision confirmed that officers must verbally inform suspects in police custody of their rights under the Fifth Amendment to the US Constitution.

The Miranda warning typically includes the following: A person may remain silent and does not have to answer police questions. If a person does tell police anything after being read the Miranda warning, that information can later be used in court. The suspect is entitled to speak with a lawyer and have an attorney present during all police questioning. If the suspect cannot afford an attorney, the jurisdiction will provide one at no expense. If a person agrees to talk to police without an attorney, he or she can stop answering questions at any time.

Should a person choose not to reply to police questioning, the decision must be shared with the officers out loud. Unless placed under arrest, a person does have the right to leave the scene of questioning. To avoid danger or false accusations, individuals should never run from police. Nor should they deliberately interfere with the official duties or responsibilities of officers. If individuals believe their constitutional rights have been abused, they can turn to organizations such as the American Civil Liberties Union for help.

The judge may allow the person to put up bail money instead, releasing that person until trial. If the accused cannot afford a lawyer, a public defender (who works for or is paid by the government) will be assigned to handle the defendant's case. All courtroom hearings are recorded by a court reporter, typically through computer transcription or audiotape.

GUILTY OR NOT GUILTY?

The arraignment is a hearing before a judge or magistrate at which the accused, in consultation with his or her attorney, enters a plea regarding the charges. If the person pleads guilty at arraignment, the court accepts the plea. The next step may be a pre-sentencing hearing. For less serious offenses, punishment may range from community service to a fine, depending on the jurisdiction. More serious cases can lead to significant prison time. In states that allow capital punishment, the death penalty may be the sentence for the most severe offenses. However, in some jurisdictions, the accused is not permitted to plead guilty in death penalty cases. Such cases must be heard by a jury or judge for a final verdict.

Defendants have the constitutional right to remain silent throughout any or all of the legal process. If this occurs, a judge must enter a plea of not guilty on behalf of the defendant. If the accused pleads not guilty in any offense, he or she has the right to full court proceedings. The defendant can choose to have a judge hear the case or instead request a jury trial under the supervision of a judge.

In actuality, only about 10 percent of all criminal cases go to trial. Most often, the two opposing sides make a plea bargain. In a plea bargain, the accused can plead guilty, perhaps to a lesser charge than the original, and accept a lesser sentence than might be received after a guilty verdict at trial. Lawyers for the defense and the prosecution may also negotiate these deals when they believe their position will be hard to prove. The prosecuting attorneys who represent the jurisdiction trying the case may agree to a deal with the defense lawyers. This is sometimes a way to avoid putting the victim through a difficult public trial. On the other hand, the prosecutor can refuse to bargain with the defense. Some courts do not allow plea deals in offenses such as sex crimes against minors. In some jurisdictions, a judge must approve any bargain. In some cases, a living victim or the grieving relatives of a deceased victim must agree to any plea negotiation.

If a person pleads not guilty, and a plea deal is not made, the next step may be a preliminary or evidentiary hearing. This is sometimes called a probable cause hearing. At this hearing, prosecuting attorneys present evidence to a judge or a grand jury. They review the evidence to determine whether there is enough proof to move forward with full prosecution of the case. Grand jury hearings are not open to the public or to the defense and do not involve a judge.

If the judge or grand jury decides the evidence presented is sufficient, a trial is scheduled. At this point, the assigned trial judge sets the ground rules for the case's courtroom proceedings. The prosecution and defense can request that the judge allow witness or expert testimony at the trial. The defendant's attorney can ask for a change of venue, moving the trial to a different location. In a new setting, the local community from which jurors would be selected may have less access to information about the case. The defense attorney can also ask the judge to exclude information about the defendant's prior criminal history or other prejudicial evidence at the trial. The judge makes these and all other decisions about the pending court proceedings. According to pre-trial rules of discovery, each side must share its evidence with the opposing attorneys. They must also reveal the testimony they plan to present. This allows both the prosecution and the defense to plan their case.

THE TRIAL

Defendants may choose to have their case heard before a judge or jury, depending on the charges and the jurisdiction. Defense attorneys may advise a client to choose a jury trial if they believe the general public will be more sympathetic. In particularly gruesome crimes, defendants may opt to have a judge hear the case. A seasoned judge may be less shocked by the offense and perhaps give a less harsh punishment than a jury might recommend.

Unless the defense agrees that a judge will hear the case, a courtroom trial begins with jury selection. The number of jurors varies by jurisdiction. Typically twelve are selected, along with one or two alternates to fill in if one of the original jurors cannot serve. During jury selection, the defense and prosecuting attorneys take turns asking potential jurors their opinions about matters related to the case. They also ask the jury candidates to talk about what they may already know or think about the situation. Both the defense and the prosecution are looking for jurors who will be sympathetic to their case. For this reason, the attorneys are legally allowed to dismiss a certain number of prospective jurors for any reason.

At the start of trial, the prosecution is the first to make an opening statement. The prosecuting attorney will introduce the government's view of how and why the crime took place. The defense attorney usually follows with an opening statement but does not have to do so. In some situations, the defense may prefer to wait until the prosecution finishes presenting all of its case. In an opening statement, the defense attorney will explain that his or her client is not responsible for the crime and why. The attorney may also provide alternate theories about what occurred. The point is to put doubt in the mind of the jurors about the prosecution's claims.

Witnesses called by the prosecution provide a range of testimony. This includes statements by any eyewitnesses, police officers, forensic scientists, or other experts. The goal of the testimony is to present a chain of events regarding the crime. The prosecution asks its witnesses to discuss the physical evidence, how it was obtained, and what it means to the case. The defense can choose to cross-examine those witnesses to try to discredit them or to challenge the evidence they presented. The prosecution can then engage in redirect examination. In this questioning, prosecution witnesses can be asked to clarify or modify statements based on issues that came up on cross-examination.

In the United States, a defendant is considered innocent until the prosecution proves its case. For this reason, the defense does not have to call a single witness or present any evidence. In addition, the defendant has a constitutional right not to testify. Typically, the defense attorney will call witnesses to help support the defendant's case. These may include eyewitnesses and perhaps expert witnesses with opinions that differ from those of the prosecution. If called, any defense witnesses may be cross-examined by the prosecution. This can be followed by redirect questioning by the defendant's attorney. During closing arguments in the case, the prosecution goes first, summing up its position. The defense then gets to argue, aiming to establish doubt in the minds of the judge or jury. The prosecution gets the last word during closing arguments because it has the burden of proving guilt.

THE VERDICT

At the end of a jury trial, the judge gives instructions to the jury about how they must conduct deliberations. The judge reminds jurors that a guilty plea can only be rendered if the jury members agree that the prosecution has proved its case beyond a reasonable doubt. The judge explains the complexities of that principle. Reasonable doubt is more than an assumption that the defendant is probably guilty. However, reasonable doubt is neither absolute certainty nor proof beyond all doubt in the minds of the jurors.

After the judge's instructions, jurors go to a private room to deliberate and render a verdict. The jury typically must reach a unanimous decision on a verdict. If they cannot, they are considered a deadlocked or hung jury, and the judge will declare a mistrial. If that happens, the prosecution can decide to try the case again, engage in plea bargaining, or dismiss the charges against the accused. However, if the verdict is a unanimous not guilty, the defendant is freed. The same applies if the case is heard by a judge who renders a not guilty verdict. The prosecution cannot request another trial.

With a guilty verdict, a judge presides over a sentencing hearing. There, the accused, the victim, or relatives and friends of either may make statements. The law sets forth what punishments a judge can choose for any given charge. Some serious crimes have a mandatory sentence. Typically, however, the judge will make a decision based on the evidence presented at trial. The judge will also review a pre-sentencing report about the convicted person's background and past offenses. The judge will consider the extent of harm inflicted on the victim and whether the accused shows remorse. If the defendant is convicted of multiple charges in a single case, the judge can decide whether the prison terms for each will be served concurrently (at the same time) or consecutively (back to back). When the death penalty is an option, the jury may have a role in making the sentencing decision. In some instances, judges with more experience with the death penalty will conduct a special hearing.

THE APPEALS PROCESS

Guilty verdicts may be appealed to a higher court if the defense believes a legal error was committed at any point in the history of the case. The basis for an appeal may involve improper police procedures during interrogation, search, or arrest. Defense attorneys may believe the judge made mistakes during the preliminary hearings or in the pre-trial motions. Either the defense or the prosecution may appeal the sentence given for a conviction. By law, a notice to appeal must be filed quickly after the conclusion of a trial. Often an attorney who specializes in appeals will take over the process. The party that is appealing (whether it is the defense or prosecution) is referred to as the appellant.

The United States has three layers of courts. The first layer includes the trial courts where cases are initially heard (also known as district courts, except in New York State, where they are called supreme courts). The next are the appellate courts where appeals are heard (also known as circuit courts). The last layer includes supreme courts, the courts of last resort. Appeals move up through the system to higher courts. The United States has twelve regional circuit appellate courts, which hear appeals for given groups of states, and one in the District of Columbia. If all else fails, some appeals move up to the US Supreme Court—the highest court in the United States—for a final decision. This entire process can take many years.

The appeal isn't another trial. It is a review of the relevant records, testimony, and evidence by a panel of three judges in the higher court to which the appeal is made. To start the appeal process, the defendant's appeals attorney provides a summary, known as a brief, to cover the main arguments for reversing the original court's decision. At an appeal, the prosecution can also present its reasons for allowing the original verdict or sentence to stand.

Appeals are rarely successful, however. This is true even in cases where the person who has been convicted and sentenced is actually innocent. Furthermore, during the appeals process, the appellant must serve any of the prison time originally sentenced. If the punishment was the death penalty, however, the execution remains on hold until all possible appeals have been heard.

"The common themes that run through these cases [of wrongful conviction]—from global problems like poverty and racial issues to criminal justice issues . . . cannot be ignored and continue to plague our criminal justice system."

—The Innocence Project, n. d.

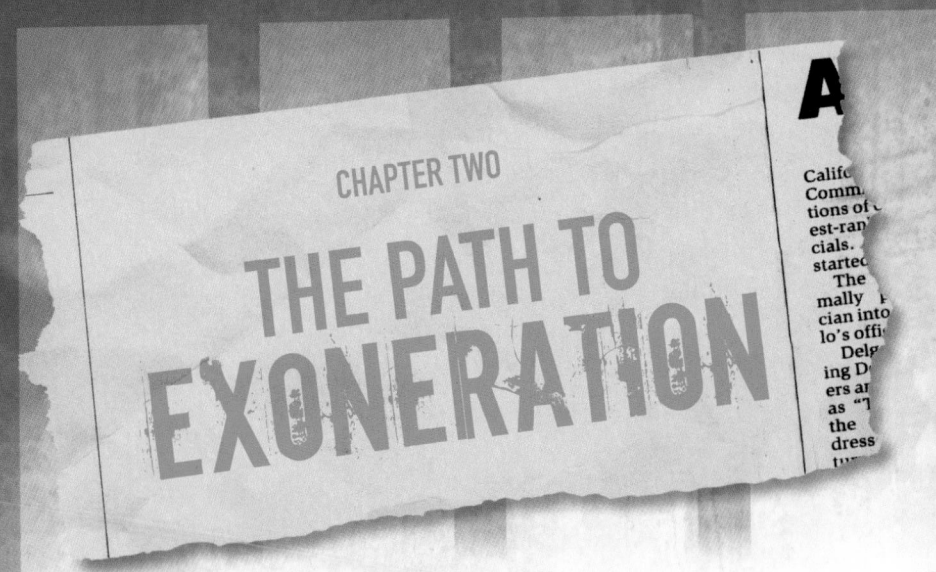

CHAPTER TWO

THE PATH TO EXONERATION

Verdicts have been questioned, challenged, and appealed throughout legal history. At present, most US states have one or more organizations dedicated to overturning false convictions. Many of these agencies are at university schools of law or criminal justice. Others are within the offices of public defenders. Some organizations take cases from across the nation. Others do not. Some have specific requirements or restrictions. For example, an agency might only take a case if the prisoner has more than a certain number of years left to serve in the sentence. Others limit the types of crimes they will consider. These groups are not devoted to cases in which people admit to their crime, even if the prisoner claims a killing was somehow justified. All groups require that the people requesting services are truly innocent of the crimes for which they were convicted.

Exoneration organizations typically do not work with those who are still suspects in criminal investigations. They work only with people who allege they have been falsely convicted by a judge or jury. Most agencies do not accept cases until all standard appeals of the conviction have been exhausted. Some exoneration groups require that physical evidence, such as DNA samples, be available for scientific analysis to help prove the person not guilty. Other organizations will accept more difficult cases in which those claiming innocence are challenging legal procedures or subjective evidence, such as eyewitness testimony.

The general process for seeking assistance begins with writing to an exoneration organization to explain the facts of a case. Some of the larger agencies have applications for assistance on their websites. This paperwork requests specific facts about the case, the conviction, and the sentence. It also asks about any new evidence that has surfaced since the trial. Review panels at the agencies evaluate this information, and their legal experts examine the issues. They conduct additional research to determine whether the case meets the organization's specific guidelines. It may take months to review the application. Once an agency accepts a case, the organization is neither the defense nor the prosecution. It is an advocate, or amicus curiae ("friend of the court"), that files an amicus brief to the appellate court. This brief is a document covering arguments and evidence for the convict's innocence.

THE INNOCENCE PROJECT

The Innocence Project is one of the first major organizations to be founded with the sole purpose of exonerating those falsely convicted. Attorneys Barry C. Scheck and Peter J. Neufeld launched the project in 1992 at the Benjamin N. Cardozo School of Law at Yeshiva University in New York. The group's interest partly stemmed from the unreliability of eyewitness testimony and related misidentifications. Its exonerations also grew from the increasing availability of forensic DNA testing to give more solid evidence of guilt or innocence. In 2004 the Innocence Project

Peter Neufeld (left) and Barry Scheck (right) founded the Innocence Project in 1992. They serve as codirectors of the project and have written several books on the topic of wrongful convictions.

became an independent nonprofit organization. The professors and students of the Cardozo School of Law are still extensively involved in each case the agency reviews and accepts.

The Innocence Project will take cases from most US states. Its current focus is on convictions in which physical evidence exists that can be tested for DNA. The organization receives more than three thousand requests each year, and the amount of time the Innocence Project is involved can last from one to ten years. As a result, the project can only accept a small number of inquiries. The attorneys and law students who work on these cases do so at no charge. Working in this way is known as pro bono publico work, a term that means "for the public good."

Most clients cannot afford the high financial costs of proving their innocence. The Innocence Project relies on donations from individuals, corporations, and foundations to pay for DNA analysis, court expenses, and any necessary travel. DNA testing costs about $1,000 per sample, and a single case may require analysis of several pieces of evidence. If a private lab performs these DNA tests, average costs for a single case can be as high as $8,500. To keep costs down, government-run labs perform some of the DNA tests for the project, often at little or no expense. According to Innocence Project data as of 2014, DNA testing exonerated 317 falsely convicted people in the United States—including eighteen who were on death row. The average time those individuals had spent behind bars before being cleared was more than thirteen years. The Innocence Project was involved in more than half of those DNA exonerations.

DNA EVIDENCE

DNA technology, based on genetic research at Leicester University in the United Kingdom, was first used in a criminal investigation in a 1986 offense. In that case, DNA comparison data exonerated Richard Buckland, a British man who had confessed to a rape and a murder he did not commit. The following year, the same technology was used to identify the real perpetrator, Colin Pitchfork.

Prior to the development of DNA testing, forensic scientists relied on serology, which is the study of bodily fluids and the various proteins they contain. Serological methods test a variety of genetically determined proteins, including those that determine a person's blood type. Some individuals also display blood proteins in other body fluids, such as saliva or semen. Serology allows for limited forensic testing on all body fluid samples. However, the proteins found in them are not unique to a single person. For example, the four major blood types (A, B, AB, and O) are shared by large groups of people. Therefore, those proteins, whether found in blood or semen, can only be properly used to exclude a suspect if that person does not have the same blood-type protein as found in a crime scene sample.

In some past criminal cases, however, serological testing was misused in forensics. It was also misrepresented to juries, resulting in wrongful convictions. Beginning in 1986, however, DNA testing allowed definitive identification of a person from body fluids and other tissues. It also permitted the reanalysis of biological samples, such as blood or semen stains, that had been stored from old crimes.

Forensic scientists can test the DNA of a living or deceased person by taking cells from the person's body. Early in DNA technology, scientists collected blood or other tissue samples. As methods improved, swabbing the inside of a person's cheek became a standard way of collecting cells for DNA testing from living individuals. In a lab, the genetic material is then extracted from either the nucleus or the mitochondria of the sample cells.

Investigators can also analyze genetic material from blood, hair, semen, saliva, skin cells, bones, and other body tissues that are found on evidence. This profile can then be compared to the DNA from known individuals (such as the suspect or the victim) to look for matches. When forensic DNA technology was first used, it required a sample of blood or semen about the size of a US quarter coin. By the 1990s, much smaller samples could be tested,

DNA

Deoxyribonucleic acid, or DNA, is a molecule that is contained in two places inside a cell—in the nucleus and in organelles known as mitochondria. Nuclear DNA comes from both of a person's parents. The mother contributes 50 percent and the father the other 50 percent. Mitochondrial DNA is inherited only from a person's mother and is identical in every direct descendant along a person's female genetic lineage. Nuclear DNA, however, is unique to each person, except for identical twins, who share the same DNA at birth.

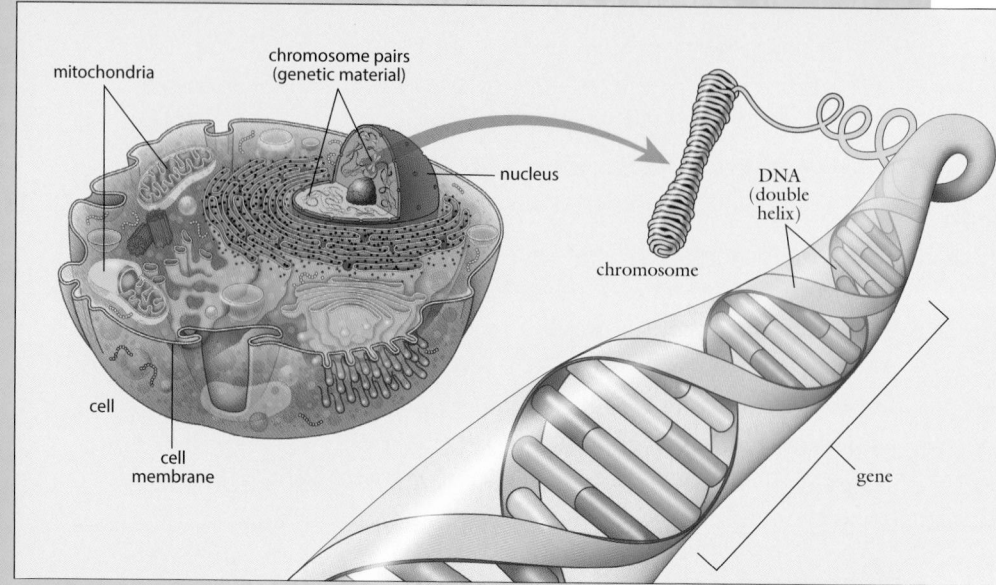

as long as they were visible. In the twenty-first century, fewer than ten cells can produce a genetic profile, including from skin cells left behind by just touching a surface.

All humans share 99.9 percent of their nuclear DNA in common. Technologies allow scientists to compare the small amount of genetic variation among people. Using chemical enzymes that act like molecular scissors, scientists can cut the variable regions of DNA into fragments. They then use a technique called electrophoresis to apply an electric current that separates those fragments by size. From there, scientists can see the resulting patterns of variation that are unique to each person. Mitochondrial DNA is tested in the same way. However, mitochondria are inherited solely from a person's mother, so all persons in a maternal line share the same mitochondrial DNA profile.

All US states require some convicted felons, such as all sex offenders, to provide a DNA sample. The sample is then tested. The encoded profile is kept in a national database for police and other legal authorities to consult for comparisons. In 2013 police began to take DNA samples from anyone arrested with probable cause for a serious crime. These DNA samples and records have the potential to solve old cases, as well as to become the basis for future exonerations.

CENTER ON WRONGFUL CONVICTIONS

Another major institution that re-examines guilty verdicts is the Center on Wrongful Convictions (CWC) at Northwestern University in Chicago, Illinois. This organization arose after the university's law school hosted a national conference in 1998 for people who had been sentenced to execution but were later exonerated. The meeting organizers wanted to use those cases to better inform the public about wrongful convictions, especially with regard to death penalty issues. Based partly on this conference and on related work, the state of Illinois abolished capital punishment in 2011. The CWC receives about 2,400 requests for assistance each year from inmates across the country.

GUILT OR INNOCENCE?

Exoneration agencies require that those who request assistance be factually innocent. All the same, statistics from the Innocence Project's DNA analyses show that people requesting testing are nearly as likely to be guilty as not guilty. Over a five-year study, DNA testing showed innocence in 43 percent of submitted cases and guilt in about 42 percent of the cases. Testing results were inconclusive in about 15 percent of requests. In more than 40 percent of those cases in which DNA did prove innocence, the same test identified the person who was actually guilty of the crime. Thus, through their work, exoneration organizations are potentially preventing perpetrators from committing other crimes, which benefits all of society.

The center's three-part mission is to represent, research, and reform. Like the Innocence Project, the CWC represents clients seeking to exonerate wrongful convictions and researches the issues that cause unjust guilty verdicts. This includes problems with unreliable eyewitness testimony and untruthful testimony from witnesses in the courtroom. It also considers cases involving poor legal representation by convicts' attorneys and misconduct on the part of police officers or forensic scientists. Like other exoneration organizations, the CWC uses the results of its studies to attempt to improve police procedures, forensic science techniques, and court processes. The center hopes to reform the system to help avoid future miscarriages of justice.

MICHIGAN INNOCENCE CLINIC

The vast majority of serious felony cases lack crime scene evidence containing biological material from which DNA can be extracted. The Michigan Innocence Clinic (MIC) at the University of

Michigan Law School in Ann Arbor was established in 2009 with a specific focus on exactly these types of cases. Wrongful convictions in non-DNA cases typically hinge on faulty eyewitness testimony, inaccurate science, or unjust legal processes. The MIC was founded on the belief that the many convictions later overturned by DNA evidence suggest unjust convictions must also exist in similar numbers in criminal cases lacking DNA evidence.

As of 2014, the MIC had taken on only eighteen requests from convicts. Seven of those people were exonerated without DNA testing. These are among the more difficult cases to reinvestigate. They involve appeals based on grounds less convincing than what DNA or fingerprint evidence can provide. As with the Innocence Project and the CWC, law students are heavily involved in the work of the MIC.

A NATIONAL DATABASE OF EXONERATIONS

In May 2012, the CWC and the MIC cofounded the National Registry of Exonerations (NRE). This database contains all known exonerations in the United States since 1989. These cases include all persons completely cleared of their charges using new evidence. By mid-2014, the NRE had listed more than 1,400 such cases. They include cases of assault, child abuse, kidnapping, arson, robbery, burglary, theft, drug possession or sale, gun possession or sale, forgery, fraud, tax evasion, traffic offense, and other crimes.

A Federal Bureau of Investigation (FBI) report found that in one year (2012) nearly 70 percent of all US arrests were of white Americans and 28 percent were black Americans. This statistic shows that black Americans—who make up about 13 percent of the US population—are arrested at higher rates than their overall representation in the nation's population. By contrast, white

Americans make up approximately 78 percent of the population and are arrested in much more proportionate measure. The NRE shows that almost half (46 percent) of the 1,325 people exonerated between 1989 and March 2014 were black Americans. These data suggest that false convictions following arrests are also higher in that racial group. Statistics from the Innocence Project show that about 70 percent of their exonerations involved individuals who are black, Hispanic, or Asian.

The FBI also reports that nearly 75 percent of arrested individuals were males. In the NRE data, males account for 92 percent of the exonerations. Studies show that males are more likely than females to commit the types of serious and violent crimes considered by exoneration agencies.

> **THE NRE SHOWS THAT ALMOST HALF (46 PERCENT) OF THE 1,325 PEOPLE EXONERATED BETWEEN 1989 AND MARCH 2014 WERE BLACK AMERICANS.**

WORLDWIDE INVOLVEMENT

Some exoneration organizations across the globe have banded together to form the Innocence Network. Its aim is to provide free legal aid and investigative services to those who claim to have been wrongfully convicted. The Innocence Network also promotes research about the causes of unjust convictions and works toward reforms. The organization launched in 2000 with ten participating exoneration groups, including the Innocence Project. By 2014 the Innocence Network numbered sixty-five separate agencies. A majority (56) of them are based in the United States or its territories. The other nine are in Australia, Canada, France, Ireland, Italy, the Netherlands, New Zealand, South Africa, and the United Kingdom.

All exoneration groups, whether in the United States or abroad, use science in the service of justice. Criminal justice studies use the behavioral sciences, such as psychology, sociology, criminology, and police science. Forensic sciences involve biology, chemistry, physics, technology, and medicine as applied to evidence of crime. Exoneration organizations also study jurisprudence and the philosophy of law in their search for improved justice and for reform of faulty laws and legal processes.

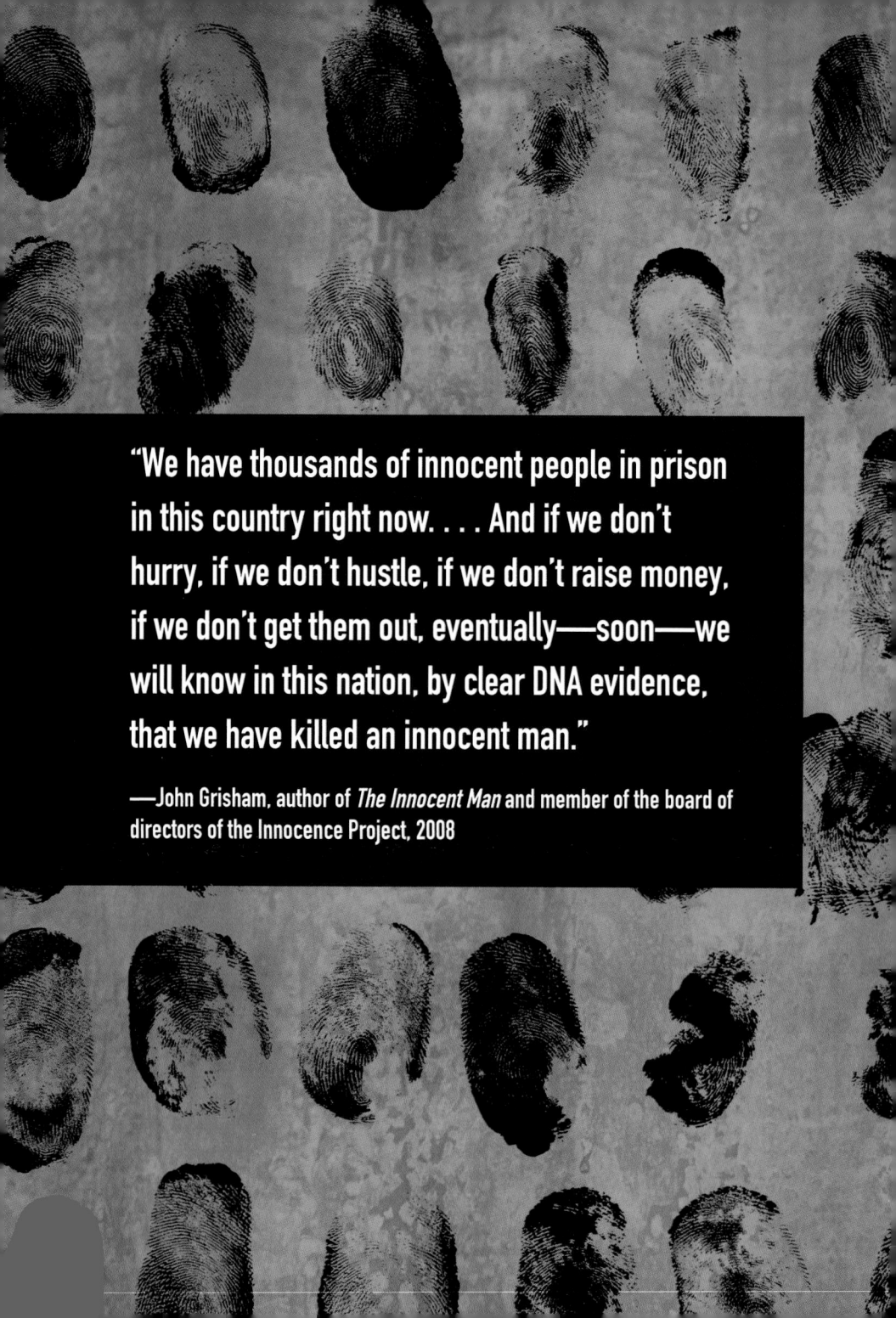

"We have thousands of innocent people in prison in this country right now. . . . And if we don't hurry, if we don't hustle, if we don't raise money, if we don't get them out, eventually—soon—we will know in this nation, by clear DNA evidence, that we have killed an innocent man."

—John Grisham, author of *The Innocent Man* and member of the board of directors of the Innocence Project, 2008

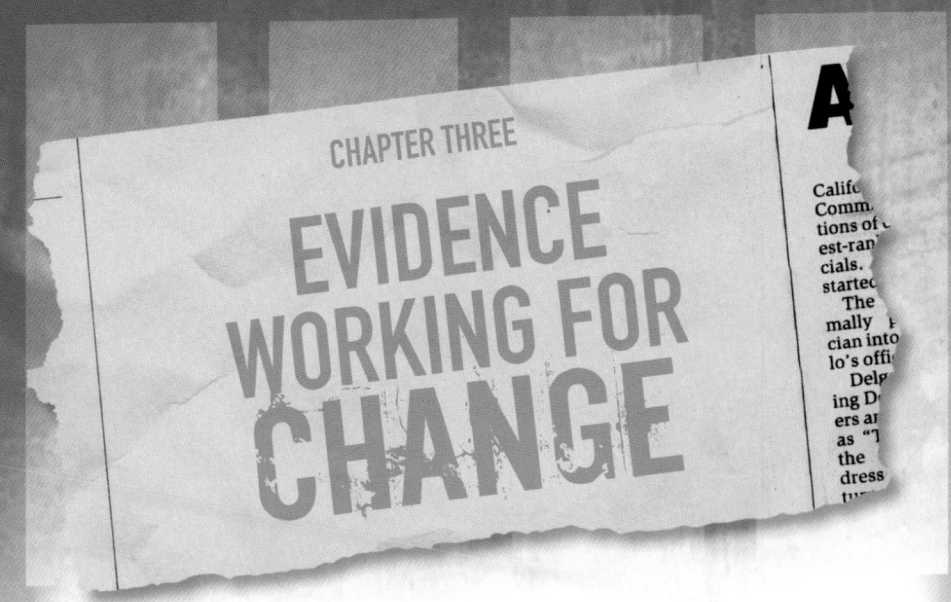

EVIDENCE WORKING FOR CHANGE

A

Calif
Comm
tions of
est-ran
cials.
started
The
mally
cian into
lo's offi
Del
ing D
ers ar
as "
the
dress

One of the guiding concepts in forensic science is that every contact leaves a trace. Set forth by French police scientist Dr. Edmond Locard about a century ago, Locard's Exchange Principle states that wherever we go and whatever we do, we leave a trail of evidence, whether we can see it or not. We also take evidence away from every interaction. In forensic terms, this means that no criminal can completely clean up all signs of a crime, and no person truly disappears without a trace. The challenge for investigators is to find that trace and to link it to a suspect.

At a crime scene, the clues left behind are sometimes obvious, such as a wall covered in blood spatter or bullet casings littering the floor. But in other cases, only minute amounts of matter—or trace evidence—is left behind or taken away. This material includes hair, skin cells, fingerprints, clothing or carpet fibers, and soil particles or plant matter on shoes or clothing.

Police, crime scene investigators, and forensic scientists must collect and treat any evidence, large or small, as if it may someday wind up in court. Most evidence does not. In many instances, the case never goes to trial or the material turns out not to be relevant to the case. Evidence may be used in court years or even decades after the crime. For this reason, officials must carefully document a chain of custody to make sure evidence holds its legal value. Materials must be securely handled and stored. The whereabouts of evidence at all points and the names of everyone who has dealt with, collected, stored, or analyzed the evidence must be carefully recorded. If suspicions arise at any point that the evidence was tampered with or that an unauthorized person has handled it, that item cannot be used in court. Improper handling of evidence or a broken chain of custody should be recognized by a judge or automatically challenged by attorneys.

THE EVIDENCE RULES

In court, evidence can include physical items such as a knife, a bloodstained jacket, rope, bones, crime scene photos, or scientific reports about fingerprint analysis or DNA testing. Evidence also includes the testimony of witnesses, law enforcement officers, and forensic experts. The purpose of all evidence presented at trial is to help the judge or jury reach a decision about the defendant's guilt or innocence. However, legal rules govern whether evidence is admissible. A case's judge determines whether or not evidence will be considered.

Rules of evidence indicate that to be admitted into court, physical items and testimony must be relevant to the case. They must also be useful in proving something about the charges under examination. For instance, if a man suspected of burglarizing a home has a gun in his car when he is caught, the presence of that gun does not establish his guilt in the burglary. The gun would not be considered as evidence unless the man used it during the burglary. The man could be charged with a separate gun offense, however. Unless the prosecuting attorney is able to clearly connect the gun to the theft—such as that it was among the stolen items— the judge would not allow the jury to hear about the gun during a trial related to the burglary charges.

In the United States, any physical evidence that makes its way to court must have been obtained by the guidelines set forth in the US Constitution. That includes the requirement of a legally executed search warrant to take evidence from private property, including the property of a suspected criminal. To do otherwise violates a person's constitutionally guaranteed right to privacy. In some cases, police are under time pressure to arrest a suspect. This may be to ensure that others are not harmed or that key evidence is not lost or destroyed. When police have probable cause that someone is guilty of a specific offense, officers are legally allowed to perform an emergency search and seizure of relevant items. If the defense later challenges probable cause, and the judge agrees,

ANY PHYSICAL EVIDENCE THAT MAKES ITS WAY TO COURT MUST HAVE BEEN OBTAINED BY.... A LEGALLY EXECUTED SEARCH WARRANT TO TAKE EVIDENCE FROM PRIVATE PROPERTY, INCLUDING THE PROPERTY OF A SUSPECTED CRIMINAL.

any evidence obtained from the emergency search will not be admissible in court.

In addition, to be admitted as evidence in a court case, materials or testimony cannot unfairly prejudice the jury. For instance, information about a defendant's prior convictions is typically not permitted at trial. Such information would likely taint the opinions of the jury. Considering other crimes in the defendant's past may cause jurors to think, "Once a criminal, always a criminal." This reaction goes against American jurisprudence, which holds that a person is innocent until proven guilty in each and every case. Prior convictions may be considered during sentencing, but only after a judge or jury concludes guilt in the case.

> INFORMATION ABOUT...PRIOR CONVICTIONS IS TYPICALLY NOT PERMITTED AT TRIAL.... CONSIDERING OTHER CRIMES IN THE DEFENDANT'S PAST MAY CAUSE JURORS TO THINK, "ONCE A CRIMINAL, ALWAYS A CRIMINAL."

Testimony given at trial also cannot be hearsay, or observations from someone who was not an eyewitness (or ear-witness) to the crime. For example, if a witness was present at a scene and heard the defendant threaten another person, the witness can tell the courtroom what he or she heard.

However, witnesses may not state what they heard from anyone other than the defendant. The accused's spouse, physician, psychologist, lawyer, or clergy member cannot be forced to testify in court about anything the defendant may have told them. Communications in these types of relationships are considered privileged matters. The US Constitution protects the conversations between people and their most trusted confidants to preserve key social bonds. In some cases, however, a judge may make exceptions to this rule about privileged communications.

SCIENCE IN THE COURTROOM

Scientific evidence, such as expert testimony about DNA results, hair analysis, or a bite-mark pattern, is governed by its own set of rules in court. By law, scientific evidence presented in a courtroom cannot be based on experimental procedures or practices. Instead, the techniques and technologies of forensic science—or any other type of science used in court—must be generally accepted as worthy by the majority of scientists in that field. This has come to mean that such tests and methods have already been published in scientific literature after having first been examined and approved by other scientists. Valid research must be conducted using standards known as controls to make sure results are accurate. Any statistical error with any method or technique must be reported and explained to the jury.

The prosecution and the defense in a criminal case may call on any scientific expert or knowledgeable authority to testify at trial. Although those witnesses may disagree in their opinions, the methods they use to reach their conclusions must still meet all legal standards. Before such persons may speak about evidence or scientific analysis to the judge or jury, however, the court must approve a witness's expertise. Typically, the judge does this by examining an expert's resumé or by asking the expert directly about his or her credentials. The court will also determine the relevance of expert witness testimony and whether the testimony will aid the jury in making their verdict. The court can do this ahead of time at pre-trial evidentiary hearings or by an examination of the expert's scientific reports. The judge can also do this at trial. If the judge decides the testimony does not meet the rules of evidence, it cannot be used at trial.

DIRECT AND CIRCUMSTANTIAL EVIDENCE

All forensic evidence is categorized as either direct or circumstantial. Both types are acceptable in court as long as they meet legal standards. They must be relevant to the case and have the potential to prove something. They must also have been collected through constitutional means.

Eyewitness testimony, such as when a witness says, "I saw her stab that man," is direct evidence in a criminal trial. The judge or jury does not have to draw a conclusion from direct testimony. They need only to accept it as true or false. All physical findings—such as DNA, fingerprints, hairs and fur, fibers, and shoeprints—are considered circumstantial evidence. Such evidence cannot definitively prove that a person committed an offense. It can only show that the suspect could have been at the scene. From circumstantial evidence, the judge or jury must draw a conclusion about the case. They often must combine multiple conclusions to develop what they believe to be a logical explanation of events that occurred during the crime.

Some traces, such as hairs and fibers, are types of circumstantial evidence that can be easily transferred from one person, pet, or object to another. They can give the false impression that the person to whom the evidence was transferred was present at a crime scene when, in fact, they may not have been. Other types of evidence, including fingerprints, are much more difficult to transfer from one place to another. All the same, they can only show that a person—or something that person touched—was present at a crime scene. They do not prove that the individual is guilty of any offense committed there.

Additionally, many items—known as class evidence—are common to a wide range of people or types of clothing. They are not distinctive enough to be tied to a single person. This can include trace evidence such as hair or more obvious evidence such as a shoeprint. For example, the color and microscopic appearance of hair can be very similar from one person to another. Clothing fibers and shoes are mass-produced. Such evidence can therefore be assigned only to a class (large grouping) of like or identical materials rather than to one specific person.

Rarely, evidence such as clothing, paper, or glass can be positively linked to a source. An example is when a tear or break from one piece can be perfectly matched, like a puzzle piece, to its adjacent piece. Occasionally, unique damage, wear, or debris on objects such as shoes or tires can also provide a confident link to crime scene evidence. Such added features can turn class evidence into individuating, or unique, evidence. Individuating evidence makes for compelling evidence in a courtroom. This information is still circumstantial, however, because the judge or jury must draw a conclusion about the case from it.

Investigators sometimes find hairs or fibers at a crime scene that appear to match known sample hairs or fibers from a suspect. In such cases, the most a reputable forensic scientist can usually say is that those items are consistent with—though not necessarily an exact match to—hair or fibers belonging to the accused. It is up to the judge or jury to draw a conclusion from that circumstantial information. On the other hand, DNA and fingerprints are

CAN DNA LEAD TO THE WRONG MAN?

In the summer of 2008, a forty-year-old teacher named Genai Coleman was killed in a suburb of Atlanta, Georgia. She had been waiting to pick up her teenage daughter at a transit station. A man approached her vehicle, shot her in the chest, and stole her car, leaving her body behind the station. Witnesses provided a description of the man. A surveillance camera from a nearby gas station also captured video of a man matching the reports. When authorities later located the stolen car, they found a cigarette butt under the driver's seat. Authorities tested saliva on the cigarette stub for DNA. They compared the results to profiles in a DNA database of persons convicted of felonies. The sample matched a man with a prior drug conviction. His name was Donald Smith.

The odds that the DNA test results were incorrect were ten billion to one. So when police apprehended Donald Smith in early 2010, they did not believe him when he said he hadn't committed the crime. Officers showed him the surveillance footage. To their surprise, Donald told them the man in the video was his identical twin brother, Ronald. He also stated that if the images were shown to the rest of the Smith family, they would confirm his claim, which they did.

Additional support for Ronald's guilt came from fingerprints found in the stolen car. Identical twins share the same DNA profile, but they do not share the same fingerprint ridge patterns. Records from Ronald Smith's cell phone usage also placed him in the vicinity where Coleman's vehicle had been abandoned. On the basis of this evidence, Ronald was arrested, charged, and brought to trial. Initially, Ronald admitted to shooting Coleman, but at trial, Ronald attempted to blame Donald. He said his own fingerprints were in the car because he had tried to help Donald clean the vehicle after the carjacking. Jurors did not believe this claim and found Ronald Smith guilty of killing Coleman. He was sentenced by the judge to spend the rest of his life in prison.

distinctive enough to be considered individuating evidence. Both, however, are still considered circumstantial because neither DNA nor fingerprints can prove on their own that the person to whom they belong is guilty of a particular crime. Only the judge or jury assigned to hear a case can make that determination as they consider other aspects of the case.

EYEWITNESS TESTIMONY

The testimony of an eyewitness is considered direct evidence because the judge or jury does not need additional information to draw a conclusion from what is stated. The statement supports a claim on its own. The listener either believes or doesn't believe what the witness says. However, people are not always honest. Eyewitnesses can also make honest mistakes, especially when asked during questioning to recall a traumatic event, such as a rape or killing.

RESEARCH HAS LONG SUGGESTED THAT EYEWITNESS OBSERVATIONS CAN BE PRONE TO SERIOUS ERROR.

Research has long suggested that eyewitness observations can be prone to serious error. Such mistakes can result in legal injustice. In 1908, for example, the German American psychologist Dr. Hugo Münsterberg wrote a landmark book entitled *On the Witness Stand: Essays on Psychology and Crime* in which he discussed how memory can fail in a person's retelling of events. He also wrote about how emotions can cloud an individual's recollection and discussed the errors eyewitnesses make when identifying suspects. In 1932 law professor Edwin Borchard of Yale Law School wrote *Convicting the Innocent,* a book about his study of false convictions. Borchard determined that eyewitness mistakes in identification of criminals were the greatest contributors to unjust guilty verdicts.

In the 1970s, psychologist Dr. Elizabeth Loftus began conducting rigorous scientific studies. She focused on how easily memory and recall are influenced. Other information and experiences can often change a person's memories. Since then Loftus has written extensively about eyewitness testimony. She has challenged its reliability and has helped to establish that direct evidence may not be straightforward and may depend greatly on circumstances.

EXONERATED: KENNY WATERS

In May 1980, the body of Katharina Reitz Brow was found in her blood-spattered Massachusetts home. Her body had more than thirty stab wounds. Some jewelry, Brow's purse, and $1,800 in cash had been stolen. Scientific testing of the blood at the crime scene showed most of it was type B, Brow's blood type. Police also found some type O blood, which they assumed belonged to the killer. Authorities eventually settled on twenty-six-year-old Kenny Waters as the prime suspect. He lived next door to Brow and worked at a

Kenny Waters (left) and his sister Betty Anne Waters (right) hold hands on the day he was exonerated in 2001. Betty Anne went to law school and became an attorney to help free her brother. Their story was made into the 2010 film **Conviction.** *Betty Anne continues to volunteer for the Innocence Project, which aided her in obtaining her brother's exoneration.*

restaurant she often visited. He also had type O blood. Police arrested Waters for the killing. Based entirely on circumstantial evidence, he was convicted in 1983 and sentenced to life in prison.

The verdict was quickly appealed, but the appeal failed. Kenny's younger sister, Betty Anne Waters, believed in his innocence and said, "Right up until that point, I really thought the system would work. I always thought only guilty people go to jail. Absolutely. That's why I was so shocked." Following that, one court appeal after another was denied.

Looking back on that time, Betty Anne said, "When Kenny was first convicted I would tell people, 'My brother's in prison and he's innocent.' And I would get that look of, 'I feel so sorry for you, Betty Anne, because he's probably guilty.' I could see the look . . . I would have thought the same thing . . . If you're in prison, you're guilty, right? Why would a jury convict you? Why would the system put you there? . . . So that's why I stopped telling people."

A SISTER'S FAITH

When Kenny attempted suicide, resulting in a month in an isolation cell, Betty Anne knew she had to take action. She made him promise not to harm himself again. In exchange for that agreement, Kenny asked her to become a lawyer and help set him free. A high school dropout, Betty Anne got her high school General Equivalency Diploma (GED) and enrolled in the local community college. After graduating with a degree in economics, Betty Anne went on to law school so she could be directly involved in her brother's case. When she learned of a new technology called DNA testing, Betty Anne knew it might be the key to freeing her brother—if the bloodstained evidence from the crime still existed.

Betty Anne Waters became her brother's attorney in 1998 and located the old evidence, including a knife and a piece of a bloodstained curtain. The evidence had been preserved in a courthouse storage area in Boston, Massachusetts. The Innocence Project agreed to take Kenny's case. The agency helped

Betty Anne arrange DNA testing on the bloodstains, which proved her brother's innocence. Kenny was released from prison in 2001, having served eighteen years behind bars for a murder he did not commit. He died in an accidental fall only six months after his release from prison, at forty-seven years of age.

Betty Anne didn't stop there, however. Her review of case documents showed that fingerprint evidence had been used during the original police investigation that led up to her brother's conviction. She was determined to find those records and learn why fingerprint evidence had not been presented in the original court case. Seven years later, Betty Anne got legal permission to search a storage unit belonging to a retired police officer involved in the case. There she found fingerprint evidence and a list of the individuals police had excluded as potential matches. Kenny Waters's name was on that list. The list proved that the police had known all along that Kenny was innocent but had held back that evidence from court. Betty Anne sued Ayer, the Massachusetts town in which Kenny had been convicted. She won her case and was awarded almost three-and-a-half million dollars.

Betty Anne assists the Innocence Project and its causes as a volunteer. She does not practice law, claiming she only went to law school to free her brother. Katharina Brow's murderer has yet to be identified.

"I couldn't believe it when the defense attorney tried to claim this was a case of mistaken identity—that I had been 'stressed' after the assault and couldn't properly identify the man who had been lying on top of me . . . I knew what I'd seen. I would never forget that face. How could I?"

—Jennifer Thompson–Cannino, rape victim and coauthor of *Picking Cotton: Our Memoir of Injustice and Redemption*, 2009

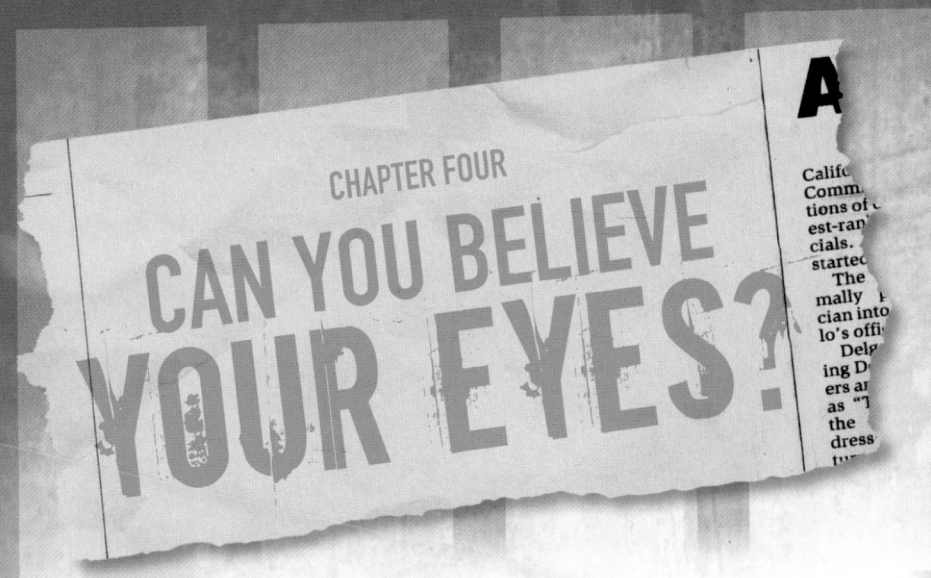

CHAPTER FOUR

CAN YOU BELIEVE YOUR EYES?

Dr. Robert Buckhout, a psychology professor at Brooklyn College in the 1970s, conducted a series of eyewitness experiments using the campus as his laboratory. In one situation, Buckhout arranged a fake assault on a fellow professor in front of almost 150 students. Then he waited seven weeks and showed the witnesses six photos of possible attackers. Forty percent of the students did identify the correct person. Yet 36 percent picked a bystander and 23 percent picked someone who hadn't even been at the scene of the attack. When Buckhout staged a purse snatching, fewer than 15 percent of the fifty-two witnesses chose the correct suspect. These early studies, and many more since, have made it clear that no two people come away from the same experience with an identical memory of it.

The Innocence Project has conducted research on successful DNA exonerations. Their studies have concluded that almost 75 percent of those wrongful convictions were due to faulty eyewitness testimony. Scientific research has revealed that our memories are not like video recorders. We create only an impression of what happened, based partly on how we were feeling at the time.

In creating a memory, a person's mind often adds other elements. These may be pieces of events that occurred at other times during which a person felt similar emotions.

TIME, PLACE, FACE, AND STRESS

Psychologists know that time is a key factor in accurate recall of memory. Memory error rates have been shown to increase within twenty minutes of an event. Experts suggest that only long-term memories—those our brain stores in a different way than casual or fleeting thoughts—can be readily recalled. Short-term memories are events that do not stick in the mind, either because they are of no significance or they do not stand out in some way. For instance, if a person passes you at the door of a convenience store and does nothing to attract your attention, you are very unlikely to recall that person's face or clothing at a later time—even if it turns out that person robbed the store.

Drugs, alcohol, and sensory or mental impairment also affect a person's ability to process and remember events or people clearly. So can factors such as poor lighting, physical distance from the event or person, or viewing point. For example, a person sitting or lying on the ground will often report a standing attacker as taller than the assailant actually is. Those who see a suspect face-on will have better recall than those who see the suspect in profile. People are also more likely to correctly recall the detailed facial features of someone from their own race. This tendency is known as cross-race identification bias. It holds true even for people who are raised in multi-racial environments. The bias reflects the brain's hardwired inability to easily distinguish among faces of those who bear less resemblance to us. Studies have also shown that people whose faces would be considered average are less memorable than those who stand out as very attractive or very unattractive.

Under certain types of stress, such as a sexual assault, the victim's brain may even alter the attacker's face as a psychological defense mechanism. In experimental studies, witnesses who were very forcefully questioned face-to-face for forty minutes misidentified their pushy interrogator almost 70 percent of the time. In a low-pressure version of that test, only 12 percent were unable to recognize the face of the questioner.

When the stress of a confrontation is created by the presence of a weapon, a weapon focus effect is introduced. If a criminal has a gun or a knife, the victim will pay more attention to the weapon than to the face of the person holding it. On the other hand, if something appeals to someone's interests in a very positive way, that person is more likely to recall that item or event. For example, a person who is very interested in cars may remember details of a vehicle more clearly than someone who is not as passionate about cars.

HOW CONFIDENT IS MEMORY?

One person's memory can be tainted by another person's memory. This is one reason witnesses in a trial are not permitted to hear each other's testimony. Younger children and the

WITNESSES WHO WERE VERY FORCEFULLY QUESTIONED FACE-TO-FACE FOR FORTY MINUTES MISIDENTIFIED THEIR PUSHY INTERROGATOR ALMOST 70 PERCENT OF THE TIME.

elderly, in particular, have been shown to have memories that are very easily influenced by suggestion, especially from those in authority. The Innocence Project has reported numerous instances in which witnesses repeatedly changed their descriptions of a suspect. Whether subconsciously or deliberately, the witnesses' new descriptions better matched what they had learned from authorities about the suspect's height, facial hair, or other features since giving their original descriptions. To avoid tainted memory recall, exoneration agencies suggest that police officers should question witnesses individually. They should also avoid suggestive and leading statements or questions. Such an approach can plant ideas into a memory that the witness didn't originally have.

People can also mistrust a first instinct, especially when they don't confidently know the answer to a question. From there—as we might do on a test, for example—we can talk ourselves into an answer, whether it is the correct answer or not. In fact, an eyewitness who is unsure of an identification in a police lineup can actually become more confident in a misidentification over time. A key factor that distinguishes a test from a police lineup, however, is that a typical multiple-choice test has a correct answer among the responses from which we select. The actual criminal may not be among the persons police show to a witness. Many variables affect a person's ability to recall a criminal's face or other aspects associated with a stressful event, leading to confusion and error.

EXONERATED: RONALD COTTON

In 1984 a black male broke into the North Carolina apartment of white college student Jennifer Thompson. While the man was raping her, Thompson consciously tried to memorize every detail of the man's face, body, and clothing. She figured that if she survived, her memories would be her best hope of making the man pay for what he had done to her. After the assault, Thompson carefully described her attacker to

In 1984 Jennifer Thompson-Cannino (right) misidentified Ronald Cotton (left) as her rapist. As a result, Cotton served nearly eleven years in prison. After his exoneration, the pair became friends and coauthored the book **Picking Cotton** *as part of their ongoing efforts to help educate the public on the causes of wrongful convictions.*

police so they could create a sketch that might help find the rapist. Officers thought her confidence would allow Thompson to pick out the right man from a photo lineup if they could find him.

Officers soon got an anonymous call that led to a man named Ronald Cotton. He worked in the area where the rape had taken place. The police handed his photograph, along with those of five other black men, to Thompson just days after the attack. She quickly pushed away four pictures and studied the remaining two. As Thompson carefully compared the pair of photos for almost five minutes, she became increasingly convinced one of the men was her rapist. She handed Ronald Cotton's photo to police and asked them how she did. They responded that she had done well. This response cemented Thompson's faith that she had chosen the right man.

Police later brought in Cotton and six other black men for a police lineup. He was the only one of the group whose photo had previously been included in the stack Jennifer had viewed. She recognized and chose him. When police again supported Thompson's selection, saying that Cotton was the same person she had identified among the photos, Ronald Cotton's fate was sealed.

At trial, Cotton maintained his innocence. But, based on Thompson's identification of him as her rapist, the jury convicted him, and he was sent to prison. There, Cotton eventually met a new inmate named Bobby Poole, who was also serving time for rape charges. Poole and Cotton looked so similar that guards and other prisoners sometimes mistook the two for each other. Cotton found out that Poole was from the same town in North Carolina where Jennifer Thompson had been raped. Cotton approached Poole and asked if he was responsible for the crime. Poole denied the accusation but later admitted to a fellow prisoner that he was Jennifer Thompson's rapist. Poole was eventually brought to court. There, Thompson swore she had never seen him, still insisting Ronald Cotton was her attacker.

"MY DNA IS NOT GOING TO BE IN THERE"

In 1994, ten years after the rape, Cotton heard about DNA testing and wondered if it might clear him.

A new pro bono attorney, Richard Rosen, had taken an interest in his case in 1992. Rosen expressed concerns about how Cotton's many failed appeals had been handled by other attorneys. Rosen also believed DNA testing would reveal the truth if crime scene samples were still available. However, Rosen warned Cotton that if he had really committed the rape and his DNA was found among the evidence, he would lose any further legal chances to pursue exoneration. Cotton replied, "I promise you I didn't do it. My DNA is not going to be in there." In time DNA testing exonerated Cotton, after eleven years in prison, and proved Bobby Poole was the true rapist.

Jennifer Thompson-Cannino and Ronald Cotton have since become friends. They tour the country, speaking out about the unreliability of eyewitness testimony and other judicial issues. They have written a book together called *Picking Cotton: Our Memoir of Injustice and Redemption.* Thompson's misidentification of Cotton and all it cost him still haunt her. Thompson wrote, "Seeing Ronald Cotton's face in the lineup, and in court, meant that his face eventually just replaced the original image of my attacker.... The standard way eyewitness evidence was collected had failed me, and because of that, I'd failed, too." Cotton is forgiving, believing that Thompson made an honest mistake influenced by flawed police line-up procedures that pushed her to identify him as the perpetrator of the crime.

"He [the policeman] taps his finger on my arm at one point. 'This is where the needle's gonna go in if you don't cooperate . . . . They're gonna send you to death row; you're gonna get executed.' This is going on for hours . . . I don't know what's going on. Everything's spinning."

—Christopher Ochoa, exoneree, speaking about his 1988 interrogation in 2005

CHAPTER FIVE

GOOD COP, BAD COP

Scientific studies highlighting the unreliability of eyewitness testimony have led to changes. They have also suggested improvements in police procedures. One suggested change is that officers show a witness a group of photos or individuals in a lineup one at a time, not all at once. With the one-at-a-time approach, the witness is less likely to compare each person or photo to the others. If the actual suspect is in the lineup, and the eyewitness has good recall, he or she will recognize a person naturally. The officer also has a duty to inform the witness that the actual criminal may not be present in the lineup or photos the witness is reviewing. These improvements can make the witness less likely to feel forced to choose a right answer.

Another reform is the blind lineup. This is a presentation of suspects in which the administrating officer does not know which member of the lineup is the actual suspect. This has been implemented because a police officer can unknowingly (or even intentionally) say things or exhibit body language that may influence the witness's decision. If the witness does pick out a member of the group, the officer should ask about and record the person's level of confidence in his or her choice. That statement would later be relayed to the judge and jury, if the case goes to court.

UNDER PRESSURE

Whether a person is talking with police or testifying on the witness stand in court, a high level of confidence does not automatically indicate truth. People can and do sometimes completely believe something that is untrue. This is different than lying. A victim or an investigating police officer may want very sincerely or feel intense pressure for a criminal to be caught. This can cause them to convince themselves or each other that the guilty party has been identified.

In some cases, questioning by the police can be so intense or hostile that suspects can mix up or begin to doubt their own story. Sometimes police pressure is so great, or the suspect's mind is so troubled, that a suspect confesses to a crime he or she did not commit. People give false confessions for a variety of reasons. These may include attention seeking, poor memory of events due to drugs or mental illness, or to protect a loved one who may be guilty. However, exoneration organizations have concluded that long hours of harsh, misleading, or threatening questions by authorities are the most frequent cause of false admissions of guilt.

A national study on wrongful convictions showed that 84 percent of false confessions happened after more than six hours of questioning. The average length of these grueling interrogations was sixteen hours. After this amount of questioning, most suspects are desperate to escape the situation, and many will confess. Often suspects confess just to buy time and much-needed rest. They tend to believe that the matter will be straightened out and their innocence revealed later in court.

All exoneration cases involving false confessions show that police did not tell the truth to the suspects about key aspects of the crime or misled them about the circumstances of events during questioning. It is not illegal for an officer to lie to a suspect during an interrogation. Lying to a witness or suspect, however, is particularly troublesome when that person is a child or is mentally handicapped. When police lie to vulnerable individuals, especially by telling them they have been abandoned or turned in by someone they trust, such individuals may give up hope. They may stop believing in themselves or think that they can go home after admitting guilt and for these reasons will falsely confess.

Police sometimes falsely tell a suspect they have absolute proof the person committed a crime. They tell the suspect he or she must have blacked out during or after the offense and doesn't remember what took place. This tactic is especially convincing to people with mental illness or drug or alcohol problems and can lead them to confess. In some instances, interrogating officers will suggest to a suspect that things will go easier if he or she admits to involvement in a killing, but that it happened in circumstances other than in cold blood. The idea of conviction for a lesser crime with a lesser punishment can be enough for people under stressful interrogation to admit to things they didn't do. Suspects cannot be told, however, that they will not be charged if they admit to a crime.

LONG HOURS OF HARSH, MISLEADING, OR THREATENING QUESTIONS BY AUTHORITIES ARE THE MOST FREQUENT CAUSE OF FALSE ADMISSIONS OF GUILT.

In a properly conducted police interrogation, questioning is directed solely to get at the truth, not to coerce a suspect into a confession. If a suspect admits guilt, an officer should ask detailed follow-up questions to make sure the suspect's account of what happened closely matches the actual crime. This will help to guard against false confessions.

THE TRUTH ABOUT LIE DETECTORS

So how do authorities uncover the truth? Polygraph machines (so-called lie detectors) and voice analyzers do not uncover lies. They indicate only a person's stress level. Stress does not automatically mean a person is lying. Anyone being questioned by police is under terrible mental pressure. Sometimes suspects who are innocent agree to a lie detector test, believing it will show they are not guilty. Yet they can begin to doubt themselves when police tell them (truthfully or not) they have failed the test. Lie detection technologies are, in fact, so flawed that the results of polygraph tests are inadmissible in most US courts. Some states do allow them, but only if both the defense and the prosecution agree to the results.

One technology, however, is extremely important during all phases of police work. As much as possible, all police procedures—whether lineups, interviews, interrogations, or confessions—should be fully recorded on video. Video recording helps protect the innocent from unacceptable police methods that contribute to false confessions and to wrongful convictions. When law enforcement uses proper processes, such recordings can also be presented in court to aid the prosecution and jury in cases of actual guilt.

EXONERATED: NICOLE HARRIS

Nicole Harris was a twenty-three-year-old woman with a degree in psychology. She worked in a nursing home. She was also the mother of two boys, five-year-old Diante and four-year-old Jaquari. On May 14, 2005, the boys' father, Sta-Von Dancy, woke from a nap in the family's apartment in Chicago, Illinois. He found Jaquari in the bedroom the two boys shared, strangled by an elastic band. The elastic had come

After almost thirty hours of grueling police questioning, Nicole Harris (above) falsely confessed to the murder of her son. Although Harris quickly took back her statement, she was convicted for the murder, based solely on the videotape of her confession.

loose from his fitted bed sheet and was wrapped around his neck ten times. Both parents tried to revive Jaquari. They called emergency medical care, which arrived too late. Police found Harris at the chapel in the hospital where her son had been pronounced dead and took her in for an interview.

A death investigator also questioned Diante, the couple's older son, who said that Jaquari liked to play Spider-Man. The boy would jump off his bed using an elastic band as a sort of spider web around his neck. The medical examiner ruled Jaquari's death an accident. Later that same day, however, Harris gave police a videotaped confession in which she admitted to strangling her son with the elastic band because he wouldn't stop crying after being punished. She was charged with first-degree murder. A trial was set for October 2005.

TRUE CONFESSIONS?

Harris informed her lawyer that she was innocent and had endured a grueling police interrogation lasting twenty-seven hours. She said officers physically and verbally abused her, shoving her and calling her a monster. She also said that police deprived her of food, water, and access to a bathroom. They gave her a polygraph test and told her she had failed it. They then coerced her into making a false confession in front of a video camera. The rest of her interrogation was not recorded.

Harris's attorney wanted the judge to allow Diante's statement about his brother's Spider-Man game as evidence. However, the prosecution claimed the boy was too young and gullible to testify. At trial, jurors saw the short video-recorded section of Harris's interrogation in which she confessed. Based primarily on the confession, she was convicted and sentenced to thirty years in prison. Six weeks after her questioning, in July 2005, Illinois law made it mandatory for police interrogations in a homicide investigation to be electronically recorded in their entirety.

Harris presented her case to the Center on Wrongful Convictions, which accepted it. At a post-conviction motion for a new trial, CWC lawyers argued that the judge had ruled incorrectly in dismissing Diante's critical testimony.

They also pointed out that Harris's defense attorney should have put the death investigator who took Diante's original statement on the witness stand. The CWC also claimed that the original trial judge had shifted the burden of proof from the prosecution to the defense. Doing so went against the laws of the state of Illinois and against accepted norms of American jurisprudence.

Ultimately, after several appeals, the Seventh Circuit Court of Appeals in Chicago gave Harris the right to a new trial. She was released in February 2013, after nearly eight years in prison. The prosecution appealed the decision of the Seventh Circuit Court to the US Supreme Court, which refused to hear the case. The prosecuting attorneys dropped the matter and did not seek a new trial. In January 2014, the Chicago court that initially prosecuted Ms. Harris issued a certificate of innocence in her name.

Steve Drizin, the legal director for the CWC, said of cases like Harris's in which there is no biological evidence, "I am hopeful that the [county] and the courts will take a close look at many of those cases in the same way they look at cases where there is DNA evidence because there are many, many more Nicole Harrises out there." As for confessing to a crime she didn't commit, Harris says, "A lot of people may not understand it. I did not understand false confessions either . . . until it happened to me." Harris could have spent the majority of the rest of her life behind bars, but with the help of the Center on Wrongful Convictions, she is a free woman.

"I can still remember looking at the jury in my trial when they heard the scientist testify. That's when I knew it was all over and I was going to prison, probably for the rest of my life. Junk science sent me to prison, but real science proved my innocence. We have to make sure that this doesn't keep happening to other people, that our system relies on solid science."

—Roy Brown, exoneree, speaking about his 1992 trial in 2009

CHAPTER SIX

BAD SCIENCE

Forensic science has proven invaluable in exonerating those who have been wrongfully convicted. However, forensic techniques, or those who misuse them, sometimes can be the reason for incorrect guilty verdicts. For example, Joyce Gilchrist was a forensic scientist with the police department in Oklahoma City, Oklahoma. She had analyzed evidence in thousands of criminal cases between 1980 and 1994. DNA testing later conclusively showed that several people her analysis and testimony had helped convict were, in reality, innocent. Gilchrist's methods included falsifying lab results and perjury (intentional lying on the witness stand). By the time her faulty methods had been exposed, eleven defendants in cases she had worked had been executed. Twelve more were sitting on death row.

Gilchrist had started her career as a forensic chemist. During two decades in the lab, she branched out to analyzing hair, carpet fibers, blood, and other evidence. She eventually became a lab supervisor. As early as 1987, some of Gilchrist's colleagues and a network of defense attorneys complained to authorities about her sloppy work. On several occasions, for example, experts for the defense had alleged in court that Gilchrist was making positive identifications of suspects based on insufficient amounts of circumstantial evidence.

Exoneration organizations, including the Innocence Project, recognized early on that some of Gilchrist's cases had resulted in wrongful convictions. They also knew that her scientific peers were accusing her of malpractice. None of the complaints were taken seriously, however. Gilchrist continued to work in the lab and was known as a very compelling witness for the prosecution. The district attorney's office regularly used her testimony to help obtain convictions, and judges allowed her to take the stand.

After a long career as a forensic scientist with the Oklahoma City Police Department, Joyce Gilchrist (above) was dismissed from her job in 2001. She had a history of falsifying evidence and making serious scientific errors in her work.

By 2001 Gilchrist's work had come under increasing scrutiny, and the FBI began to study her casework. In six of the first eight cases it examined, the FBI concluded that Gilchrist had committed scientific errors or had overstated what could be properly concluded from her testing. Follow-up studies discovered Gilchrist had sometimes failed to perform tests that might have cleared the accused. She had also withheld important evidence from the defense. Further investigation showed that some evidence necessary to appeal convictions was mysteriously and improperly missing from her lab. Some of it had even been destroyed.

For this reason, those who were falsely convicted because of her work may never have a chance to clear their guilty verdicts. In all, Gilchrist may have been negligent or deceitful in more than 1,875 instances in the 3,000 cases in which she participated.

WHAT IS GOOD SCIENCE?

Rules of evidence require that judges and juries consider the worth of the scientific evidence attorneys present in court. This helps ensure that "junk science" does not make its way into the courtroom. Good science can be recognized in several ways. Proper science must be developed using the scientific method. This means creating a solid hypothesis and testing the idea using controlled experimentation. An example of a hypothesis might be: If two bullets are fired by the same gun, they will show the same pattern of microscopic marks known as striations. To support the hypothesis, researchers would carry out many repeated experimental trials using bullets fired from the same gun. They would then compare the striations on those bullets to striations on identical bullets fired from different guns. Quality science does not end there. It must then be presented to other scientists for their evaluation and testing. When a group of scientific peers has agreed that a method such as bullet comparison is valid, it is accepted as reliable science. Only then can such methods be properly used to analyze similar forensic evidence in a criminal case.

The FBI began relying solely on DNA as individuating evidence in 1999. However, only 5 to 10 percent of all criminal cases have any DNA-containing biological material to test. For example, cases such as drive-by shootings typically leave no physical trace of the perpetrator at the crime scene. In other offenses, forensic investigators may have used poor evidence collection or storage techniques. Evidence may have been destroyed before its importance was recognized, especially prior to the development of DNA technology. While some of these issues can be addressed with improvements in forensic science, others cannot.

FORENSIC SCIENCE GOES ON TRIAL

As experts learn more or as techniques fail, the standards for judging reliable science can change. For example, many longstanding methods are under increasing scrutiny. They include polygraphs and related lie detection methods, microscopic hair comparisons, bite-mark analyses, burn patterns in arson cases, handwriting examination, and bullet comparisons. In fact, in 2005, the US Congress appointed the National Academy of Sciences (NAS) to thoroughly review forensic science practices. The resulting 350-page NAS report from 2009 concluded that DNA is the only forensic method that can consistently and with a high rate of accuracy connect evidence to a specific person.

Stemming from the NAS report, the FBI began a review in 2013 of more than two thousand of its own cases. The FBI is looking at situations in which microscopic hair comparisons were used to identify and convict suspects between 1985 and 2000. The FBI is using DNA technology to check the accuracy of its hair matches in these old cases. DNA can be extracted from hair shafts, even those that are decades old. The DNA testing will prove whether the microscopic hair matches were correct or not. The FBI will then be able to scientifically document the reliability of microscopic hair comparisons. These types of rigorous tests may shed further doubt on methods formerly considered accurate. If so, they may form the groundwork for future exonerations.

The NAS report also found fault with some areas of forensic

career preparation and training. It also uncovered a lack of established procedures by which forensic scientists are qualified. Some of this is related to the rapid growth of forensic science and technology in the late twentieth century. Many practitioners rose up through the ranks without proper education and competency testing. They got jobs that agencies were desperate to fill. Yet forensic analysts who are not well trained can misinterpret results or boost their conclusions to levels that cannot be scientifically supported. Their testimony can sway jurors, especially those who lack science education. Some jurors may believe that simply because something sounds scientific, it must be accurate.

In addition, the NAS report identified a lack of centralized oversight for forensic labs in the United States. The lack of a single system of lab protocols has led to inconsistencies in forensic analyses. As a remedy, the NAS and the Innocence Project both support the creation of an independent federal institution to conduct research on forensic methods and their reliability. The institution would establish and enforce standards for forensic science, from the crime scene to the courtroom, including all laboratory analyses.

About half of the cases successfully overturned through the intervention of the Innocence Project included faulty forensic science. Any human endeavor is open to error. All forensic testing that relies heavily on subjective, opinion-based interpretation is vulnerable to human bias. This does not mean all forensic methods are wrong or based on bad science. Many experts argue that vague and poorly defined forensic standards—along with poor practitioners seeking fame or to advance their careers—are far more to blame for mistakes than are flawed methods.

EXONERATED: JAMES E. RICHARDSON JR.

James Richardson was outside his father's West Virginia home in May 1989 when he realized a neighbor's house was on fire. He broke down the neighbor's door and saved a three-year-old girl from the burning house. After the fire was extinguished, the body of the child's mother, Kelli Gilfilin, was discovered. She had been tied up, raped, and beaten to death.

At first, thirty-three-year-old Richardson received a hero's praise. But he was quickly arrested and charged with arson, rape, and murder. Three other suspects were dismissed based on forensic serology tests. The investigation centered on Richardson. He was thought to have raped and killed Gilfilin, set the fire to cover the crime, and then staged the rescue of the child.

Two months after the crime, forensic scientist Fred Zain of the West Virginia State Police Crime Lab testified in court. He said that proteins in semen on the victim not only connected Richardson to the crime but also excluded the other three men as suspects. A jury was presented this serological class evidence (which turned out to be false) even though more precise individuating DNA testing was available at the time. They convicted Richardson to life in prison with no chance of parole.

THE CASE AGAINST ZAIN

Ten years later, a different criminal case was building. The states of West Virginia and Texas had brought charges against Zain for allegedly falsifying data. They also charged that Zain did not actually conduct some tests he claimed to have undertaken during a sixteen-year career at various state crime labs. Zain had earned poor grades as he pursued his college chemistry degree and had lied about his credentials. Yet somehow he ended up working on hundreds of cases spanning a dozen states. He had a history of being fired by one agency, only to be hired by another.

In analyzing the semen in Gilfilin's murder, Zain had not even considered or examined the victim's body fluid proteins. The victim's own proteins could have completely masked those of the suspect, making Zain's determination about Richardson's guilt invalid. George Castelle, the chief public defender in Charleston, West Virginia, said Zain's methods amounted to "a blueprint on how to convict an innocent person."

A reinvestigation of Richardson's case also showed that police had not revealed that a bloodstained flashlight had been found at the crime scene. DNA testing showed that the blood on the flashlight belonged neither to Richardson nor to the victim. It belonged to a third person (yet to be identified). Records also showed that the three-year-old witness to her mother's murder had told police that she had seen part of the attack on her mother and that Richardson was not the man who did it. That evidence was not presented at trial.

Following indictments against Zain, Richardson's conviction was set aside in 1996 based on the state's reinvestigation of his case. Richardson was released from prison and assigned to home confinement, pending further investigation. Home confinement ended in 1998, and all charges against him were dropped in 1999. Richardson married and had a son, to whom he gave the middle name Castelle, after the public defender who pursued the allegations against Zain.

In a later legal settlement, the state of West Virginia awarded Richardson two million dollars for his wrongful conviction and for the seven years he had spent in prison. Zain's trial was indefinitely postponed when he developed cancer. He died in 2002. Richardson, a true hero for saving Kelli Gilfilin's three-year-old daughter, died of a heart attack in 2011.

"The history of the snitch is long and inglorious. . . . Their motives, then as now, were unholy. . . . When the criminal justice system offers witnesses incentives to lie, they will."

—Center on Wrongful Convictions, Northwestern University, 2004

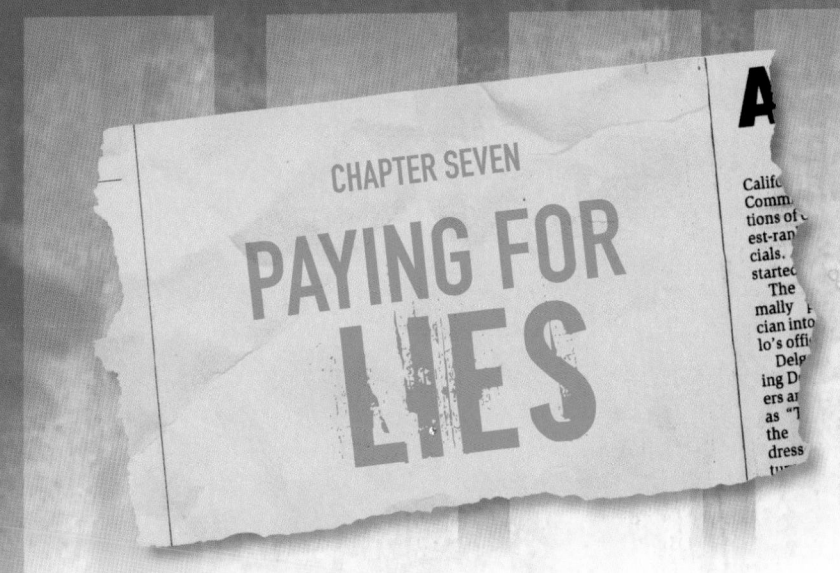

CHAPTER SEVEN

PAYING FOR LIES

Califo
Comm.
tions of u
est-ran
cials.
started
The
mally r
cian into
lo's offi
Delp
ing D
ers ar
as "T
the
dress

Prosecuting attorneys and police commonly rely on giving rewards or incentives for testimony. In exchange for information about a suspect, an imprisoned criminal may be able to receive a reduced sentence or earn other privileges. Sometimes the prosecutor's office pays cash rewards to informants or to others willing to testify in a case. This can encourage people to make false statements about what they've heard. They may also invent phony eyewitness accounts of events.

The informants can include fellow inmates, who often claim that a suspect confessed to them. They may be members of organized crime networks not currently in jail but who want to see a member of a rival gang punished or out of the way. Angry spouses, ex-lovers, estranged family members, or other enemies may also lie about innocent persons just to see them put behind bars. Perjurers can include a co-defendant (someone who has been charged with the same crime). In such cases, one of the defendants may lie to the police, judge, or jury to implicate the other innocent defendant and to remove blame from him or herself. Agreeing to testify against a co-defendant may also be part of a plea bargain.

Overzealous law enforcement officers, eager to obtain a guilty verdict, sometimes feed jailhouse snitches insider information about a case that is not publicly available. These informants may have pending charges of their own for which they want to avoid prosecution. They will agree to testify in court about the information police feed to them as if it was their own knowledge. Jurors tend to view this information, which seems like something only an eyewitness would know, as truthful and therefore compelling.

Statistics from the National Registry of Exonerations show that perjured testimony and false accusations occurred in 56 percent of more than 1,300 recorded exonerations. Perjured testimony is most common in cases involving homicide and child sexual abuse. In the wrongful convictions of homicide cases, 65 percent involved testimony that was later discovered to be false. In some cases, the testimony was found to have been the result of police prompting of witnesses. In 81 percent of exonerated allegations of childhood sexual abuse, victims have changed their stories. They admit that sex abuse did not actually take place but that family members or others in charge of their welfare had pressured or coached them to make a false accusation.

AVOIDING PERJURED TESTIMONY

It is illegal in the United States for a criminal defendant to tamper with the testimony of a witness. This is true whether the tampering is to prevent or to promote testimony. Yet the practice of paying for testimony is widespread among government prosecutors, defense attorneys, and other authorities. Judge Paul J. Kelly Jr. of the US Court of Appeals for the Tenth Circuit said of one appeal, "If justice is perverted when a criminal defendant seeks to buy testimony from a witness, it is no less perverted when the government does so. . . . The judicial process is tainted and justice is cheapened when factual testimony is purchased, whether with leniency or money."

Exoneration organizations recommend that law enforcement agents record any interviews with potential informants in full. This will show that police have not provided details to which the cooperating witness later testifies. Agencies also recommend that jailhouse informants wear a hidden wire (recording device) during pre-arranged conversations with fellow inmates or with other criminals they claim have confessed to crimes. During these secretly recorded conversations, the informant should be directed by authorities to ask questions that capture specific and unique follow-up details about any confession they claim to have heard. Without this proof, testimony related to jailhouse conversations should not be permitted in court. Exoneration agencies also point out that situations involving incentivized testimony are highly suspicious if informant statements are the only evidence, either direct or circumstantial, in a criminal case. A strong, factual case must always include a much wider range of evidence.

Prosecutors are legally required to tell the defense about any deals they have made with witnesses. In addition, exoneration organizations suggest that police report to the judge and jury when any incentives are offered for testimony. This would allow judges and jurors to weigh the source of and potential motives for such information in their decision-making process. Judges are also encouraged to explain the risks and known problems with informant testimony during jury instructions. Perjured testimony—whether rewarded or not—has caused too many innocent individuals to pay for lies with years behind bars.

EXONERATED: ELROY "LUCKY" JONES

In early June 2006, several people outside a drug-infested apartment building in Detroit, Michigan, heard gunshots from inside. As they watched, a man named Matenis Carter ran away from the scene. Another man shoved an AK-47 rifle out of a second-story window in the building and began firing at him. A third man, Cleo McDougal, lay shot to death inside the apartment. Carter was the brother of the victim and denied knowing the shooter. A few days later, however, Carter told police the gunman was Elroy "Lucky" Jones, a twenty-six-year-old man he knew. Jones had a criminal record that included drug convictions and an assault. As a result of Carter's information, Jones was charged with first-degree murder and with other offenses related to the shootout at the apartment building.

At the preliminary hearing, officers brought Jones in before a male eyewitness who lived in the apartment across the street from the murder. Police and prosecutors wanted to see if the eyewitness would identify Jones as the shooter. Jones's mother reported, "I watched the police bring in a young man that was their witness and as soon as he seen my son, he looked, and then he mouthed to the police, 'that's not him.'" Still, the police and prosecutor pressed on with the charges against Jones. At trial, that same witness took the stand for the defense, stating that the man who had been shooting out of the window was not Jones. The witness claimed he was sure the defendant was much larger than the actual gunman. He stated the shooter was small enough to get much of his body out of the apartment window as he was firing the gun. The male witness also testified that a police officer had pressured him during a lineup to say Jones was the gunman.

In addition to questionable eyewitness testimony, physical evidence did not connect Jones to the crime. The only person to say Jones was the shooter was the dead man's brother. All the same, Jones was convicted in late 2006 and was sentenced to life behind bars without parole. An appeal was impossible, however, because someone stole the tapes of the court proceedings from the court reporter's car before she could transcribe them. Unable to assess the information presented at the original court case, the Michigan Court of Appeals reversed Jones's conviction in 2008. By Michigan law, the overturned conviction paved the way for a new trial. At his second trial in 2008, Jones was again convicted and handed a life sentence.

AN INFORMANT PAYS OFF

In 2011, while federal officers were investigating a totally unrelated matter, they interviewed a man who informed them he had driven the real gunman to the Detroit apartment in 2006. This alleged shooter was in prison on drug charges. Detroit police arranged a lineup with the new suspect for some of the original witnesses to the crime. Almost all of them identified the new man as the gunman from the 2006 murder. In fact, one of the witnesses claimed he had identified the man as the killer to authorities in 2006, but at that time they would not listen. After learning of the new information, the police began working to free Jones and to find the real criminal. Deputy Chief David Levalley said, "If we put the wrong person in prison and we find out about it later on, and we don't take the necessary steps to correct that, then our credibility going forward is tarnished."

Based on the new evidence, Jones's attorney filed a motion to overturn his conviction in Michigan's Wayne County Circuit Court. Once again, the court set aside Jones's conviction and ordered another new trial. However, the prosecutor's office decided not to pursue a third trial, and in early 2014, Elroy Jones finally got lucky. He was released from prison, after seven years, with all charges dropped.

"I thought they were there to help . . . I really thought, 'You know what? I'm innocent and there is no way I'm going to prison.' And I didn't worry. All the way through trial I wasn't worried. I wasn't worried until the day they came back and said, 'Guilty.' Then I got worried real fast."

—Peter Rose, exoneree, reflecting on his 1995 trial in 2005

CHAPTER EIGHT

POOR LAWYERING AND UNJUST JUSTICES

Once a criminal suspect has been arrested, he or she has the right to an attorney. But that right doesn't guarantee an outstanding lawyer, or even a satisfactory one. Studies of exonerations have shown that poor legal counsel has often contributed greatly toward wrongful guilty verdicts.

Defense attorneys may fail their clients in various ways. An incompetent lawyer may neglect to thoroughly investigate or present the defendant's story. The attorney may ignore an alibi that would show the accused was nowhere near the scene of the crime. Bad lawyering has also failed to expose faulty science and poor police procedures. Exoneration organizations cite examples of defense attorneys who did not show up for court or who were asleep or drunk during courtroom proceedings.

Exoneration agency research shows that faulty lawyering often lies in what a defense attorney does not do in a case, rather than what he or she actually does. But it is difficult to uncover and right the wrongs of a poor legal defense, even when an unjust conviction is up for appeal. This is because the standard appeals process is limited to what took place at a previous trial. It is not based on new evidence that may be discovered or that was previously withheld. The appeals attorney or an exoneration agency may want to present new evidence to an appellate court, such as information the trial lawyer neglected in the case. But to do so, an attorney must first submit a legal brief explaining why the new evidence should be permitted after the original trial. The appellate court must then agree to the motion to hear the new evidence before it can be considered.

Prosecuting attorneys who abuse their authority can also contribute to wrongful convictions. In 2013 one federal appeals judge remarked on what he saw as an epidemic of prosecuting attorneys purposely withholding important evidence they know would aid the defense. This is against the rules of discovery in a criminal case. In addition, both prosecutors and defense attorneys sometimes attempt to include court testimony of individuals they know to be lying. Some attorneys also use experts they know are unethical or incompetent. In such cases, an attorney's zeal for winning a case can overcome the obligation to uphold justice. It is up to the judge to try to recognize these tactics and prevent them from tainting the legal case.

ERRORS OF JUDGMENT

Judges are attorneys who, after years of experience (usually as a prosecutor), are appointed or elected to their position. They decide cases brought before a court of law. A good judge is completely familiar with all legal processes. Like anyone else, though, a judge can make mistakes. Judges can also be guilty of official misconduct if they ignore policies and procedures. If a jury is deadlocked, for example—unable to make a decision about guilt or innocence—a judge is legally required to declare a mistrial. This leads to a new trial. However, some judges may tell a deadlocked jury they must continue to deliberate no matter what. Judges may also deny legal motions they know should be granted or hold back evidence that should be allowed.

Judges are not advocates for one side or the other. They are more like referees who must try to avoid all bias and fairly apply the law. Trial judges evaluate evidence and questions of fact. Appellate judges, on the other hand, are experts in examining questions of law. The appeals process is a way to allow other judges to examine and re-evaluate a court case. Appellate judges will look for problems that may have occurred at trial, including judicial errors or bias. Rather than focusing on evidence, appeal courts review how well the law was applied by a previous trial judge when hearing a case. When appellate courts find legal mistakes or negligence, they must reverse or amend the original trial court's decision. The criminal justice system is responsible for identifying patterns of misconduct—such as bias, corruption, or incompetence— and should push to remove unethical or ineffective lawyers and judges from their positions.

THE CRIMINAL JUSTICE SYSTEM IS RESPONSIBLE FOR IDENTIFYING PATTERNS OF MISCONDUCT—SUCH AS BIAS, CORRUPTION, OR INCOMPETENCE.

PREVENTING FUTURE LEGAL MISCONDUCT

The Innocence Project reports that misconduct on the part of the prosecution was behind nearly half of all its cases resulting in exoneration. These included cases in which the prosecution knew of—but concealed—evidence that would have supported the defendant's innocence. But the Innocence Project accepts only cases for which DNA evidence exists. For this reason, its work likely represents only a small fraction of wrongful convictions based on inadequate legal defense.

The types of legal issues that promote wrongful convictions are complex. In many parts of the country, funding is not sufficient to provide salaries for enough highly qualified public defenders to handle the area's caseload. When overworked, lawyers may not have the time to fully study each case and prepare a solid defense. Research also suggests that defense attorneys who are incompetent, prosecutors who engage in misconduct, and judges with track records of mistakes are not routinely removed from office and/or punished for their misdeeds. The same is often true for police who misuse their authority. To reduce the number of wrongful convictions associated with legal errors, exoneration agencies stress the need to address all such issues. They also suggest the need for strict standards of ongoing training to help ensure competence among attorneys and police.

EXONERATED: EARL WASHINGTON JR.

In 1983 twenty-two-year-old Earl Washington Jr. was picked up by police in his Fauquier County, Virginia, neighborhood. He was accused of breaking into the home of Helen Weeks, an elderly woman, earlier that same morning and hitting her with a chair. Police questioned Washington for two days before claiming he had confessed to the attack. He also admitted to five unsolved

Earl Washington Jr. (center) walks with his legal team, Marie Deans (left) and Barry Weinstein (right) on their way to a 2001 press conference after Washington's exoneration. During police interrogation in 1983, he had falsely confessed to rape and murder.

crimes in several nearby areas. He would not be free again until 2001.

At the time, Washington's estimated intelligence quotient (IQ) was 69. The clinical psychologist who tested Washington classified him as having mild mental retardation (now called intellectual disability). Worldwide, an average IQ is around 100, and only 2.2 percent of the population has a score below 70. To be considered competent or fit to stand trial, defendants must be deemed able to understand the nature of the legal charges against them. They must also be able to understand the sentencing they may face. In addition, they must be judged able to assist their attorneys in their own defense. This includes the ability to recall the facts of the case and to testify on their own behalf, if desired. In cases where the judge suspects intellectual disability, the court will order a psychological assessment of a defendant.

Washington was indicted for attacking Weeks, and he later pled guilty in that case. When witnesses in four of the five unresolved crimes to which Washington had confessed did not recognize him, those charges were eventually dropped. The fifth crime, for which Washington had admitted guilt, was the unsolved rape and murder of Rebecca Lynn Williams, a nineteen-year-old mother of three young children. About a year before Washington's arrest, Williams had been stabbed multiple times in nearby Culpepper County, Virginia. Before losing consciousness, the victim had told her husband that one black man had attacked her. During pre-trial hearings in the case, a Culpepper County Circuit Court judge ruled Washington competent to stand trial for the rape-murder. The judge also determined that police had properly taken Washington's confession.

By the time of the trial, both the defense and the prosecution had the psychological report and the full transcript of the police interrogation of Washington. It showed that Washington did not know the rape-murder victim's race or address. He also did not know that she had been raped before being killed. Washington's confession stated that he had stabbed her two or three times. In fact, the autopsy report documented thirty-eight wounds. Washington was only able to identify the apartment where the attack had taken place after police took him there three times and pointed it out to him. In addition, serological protein testing on a semen sample from the crime scene did not match Washington's proteins. The lab report had been altered to falsely suggest the testing was inconclusive.

"THEY DIDN'T PUT ON MUCH OF A CASE"

Washington had a very poor defense attorney who had never tried a death penalty case. The attorney did not build a strong case of innocence for his client despite the wealth of information available to him. For example, he did not present to the jury the forensic psychologist's report of Washington's strong desire to please others, particularly authority figures. Nor did he expose that Washington functioned at what was judged to be the mental level of a ten-year-old child. Instead, the only psychological evaluation presented to the jury came from the prosecution—not the defense. It stated only that Washington was competent to stand trial. Juror Jacob Dodson later said, "I figured the defense was saying he was guilty, too, because they didn't put on much of a case."

The court case lasted less than five hours, including jury deliberations. The jury found Washington guilty. At the sentencing hearing, he received the death penalty. His defense attorney did not argue against the punishment. The US Supreme Court has since ruled that those with intellectual disability cannot be sentenced to death, as it violates the US Constitution's ban on cruel and unusual punishment.

In a federal appeal, a panel of judges established the lack of proper legal representation in Washington's case. All the same, the panel refused to reverse the conviction. In prison, Washington was only nine days away from death when a last-minute appeal delayed his execution. A concerned fellow death row inmate—Joseph Giarratano—had contacted legal authorities about Washington's case. He instituted a lawsuit on Washington's behalf, citing the lack of proper legal representation. The inmate's actions led to the appeal that postponed Washington's execution and ultimately caused the Innocence Project to accept his case.

In October 1993, new DNA testing showed that the semen found on the victim's body could not have been Washington's. However, the law in Virginia at the time stated that to be considered in a case, new evidence had to be introduced within twenty-one days after trial. (That law has since been repealed based on this case.) So on his last day in office, the governor of Virginia reduced Washington's sentence from execution to life in prison. Six years later, a new governor requested additional DNA testing. Testing took some time, but the improved technology revealed two distinct DNA profiles, neither of which belonged to Washington. The governor pardoned Washington of murder in October 2000. However, he was not freed until more than four months later, when he reached the release date of his sentence for assaulting Weeks. By the time he was finally freed in February 2001, Washington had served more than seventeen years behind bars.

In 2006, using the DNA testing results obtained in 2000, authorities were able to identify and to indict the actual perpetrator of the rape-murder—Kenneth M. Tinsley. He was already in prison for another rape committed after the attack on Williams. (The source of the second DNA profile from the case has still not been identified). Washington and his attorneys filed a lawsuit against the state of Virginia, and he was awarded more than two million dollars in damages in 2006.

CHAPTER NINE

WHERE DO WE GO FROM HERE?

The year 2012 marked a milestone in the history of innocence-advocacy organizations. The National Registry of Exonerations reported that, for the first time, police or prosecutors aided in or were actually responsible for initiating more than half (54 percent) of that year's sixty-three overturned convictions. This shift shows the increasing willingness of the legal system to police itself by recognizing and correcting injustice, regardless of its cause. Cooperation from officials, however, is still least likely in exoneration attempts for cases that are highly publicized. It is also unlikely in cases in which the probable legal errors are enormous. Grave mistakes are often the hardest to admit. They can bring even more scrutiny and public disapproval upon the authorities responsible.

The NRE also indicated an increase in 2012 of overturned convictions for those who were innocent but who had actually pled guilty. When the total registry data (from 1989 to 2014) is considered, 11 percent of those exonerated had originally pled guilty to crimes they did not commit. The remaining 89 percent

"There is no way to tell from [past] cases whether we are getting better at avoiding wrongful convictions in the first place. It does seem, however, that we are working harder to identify the mistakes we made years ago and that we are catching more of them. If we are also learning from those tragic errors that have come to light, that would be a big step in the right direction."

—National Registry of Exonerations, 2014

had pled not guilty but were convicted at trial by juries or judges. This increasing trend in overturning convictions of those who had pled guilty is thought to reflect an environment of greater openness. Authorities are more readily re-examining cases where the defendant opted for (or was pressured into) a plea bargain rather than risk a more severe penalty at trial.

EXONERATIONS AND THE DEATH PENALTY

As of 2014, thirty-two states permit the death penalty as a sentencing option. So do the federal government and the US military. Eighteen states and the District of Columbia have abolished it. Only 8 percent of the cases in the NRE are those of convictions that led to death sentences. This is significant, however, since only a small fraction of all guilty verdicts result in a sentence of execution (less than 1/100th of 1 percent). Overall, death sentences have decreased in the United States. In the decade from 1991 to 2000, the average was more than 280 per year. From 2001 to 2010, that average dropped to around 123 per year. Between 2011 and the end of 2013, the average number of death sentences each year in the United States fell to 80. This decrease may be in part because exonerations—especially those in which DNA testing has led to the real perpetrator—have highlighted a range of mistakes. This includes faulty eyewitness testimony, controversial police procedures, flawed forensic science, and other legal errors.

If conducted properly and reported honestly, DNA testing provides the legal system with more accurate identification of criminal perpetrators even before court proceedings. This results in fewer false convictions now than in the past. For this reason, the number of wrongful convictions overturned by DNA testing continues to fall slowly. However, non-DNA exonerations, which

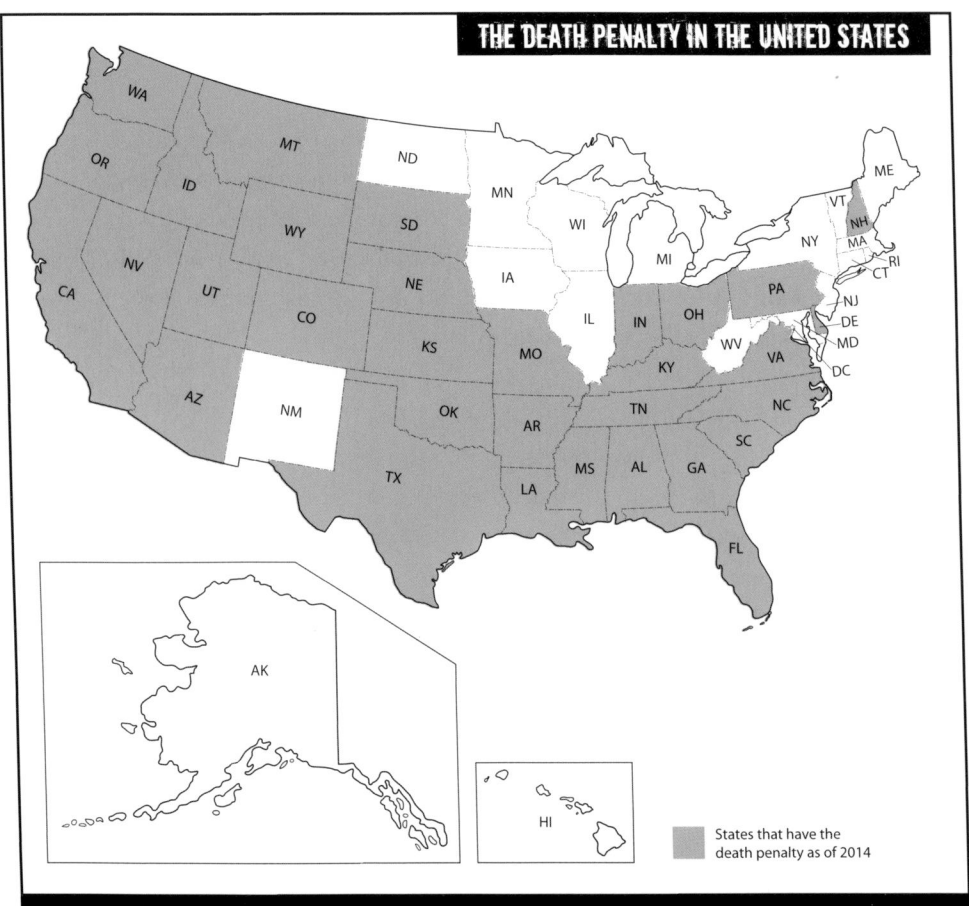

States that have the death penalty as of 2014

This map shows the states that currently have the death penalty and those that do not.

are more difficult to achieve, are on the rise. They will make up the majority of future exonerations because most cases have no biological evidence to test.

A RECORD YEAR

According to the National Registry of Exonerations, 2013 was a record year in the United States. A total of eighty-seven exonerations were recorded by the time the registry's 2013 annual report was finalized. About one-fifth of those were aided by DNA analysis. Nearly one-third involved alleged crimes that never even took place. These were mostly false allegations of sexual assault or drug offenses for which individuals had been framed. One-third of the total exonerations were for crimes other than homicide or rape. Almost half (46 percent) were in murder cases, one of which overturned a death-row sentence.

Nearly half (forty-three) of the convictions overturned in 2013 occurred in just five states: Texas, Illinois, New York, Washington, and California. This may mean some geographic areas are working harder than others to fight injustices or that they are catching up on a larger number of overdue exonerations. It may also be that the likelihood of error is greater overall in states with larger populations and with more legal cases than other, smaller states.

COMPENSATING FOR LOST TIME

Exonerations can be made during a person's lifetime or posthumously, after the wrongfully convicted person is dead. Exonerations clear a person's name, bring the family justice, and help society and the legal system learn from past mistakes. But what about those men and women who finally walk free after years of being wrongfully held in prison? The media captures tearful reunions with family members, attorneys and exoneration organizations receive heartfelt thanks, and a tragic chapter in the lives of those who have been falsely convicted closes.

The lost years can never be reclaimed, however. Of the first 250 exonerations made through DNA testing, 21 percent of the individuals were younger than twenty-one years of age (6 percent were younger than age eighteen). The average age at conviction was twenty-seven; the average age at exoneration was forty-two.

For many people, these are among the most productive years of life. Some exonerated individuals missed the opportunity to get married or have children. Others suffered in prison while their children grew up or loved ones died. Many of the wrongfully convicted individuals were incarcerated during formative career years. They lost out on a chance to enhance their skills and contribute to society.

To help avoid future mistakes in federal criminal cases, as well as to aid the victims of federal crimes, the US Congress overwhelmingly passed the Justice for All Act into law in 2004. Among other things, this legislation provided federal funding for forensic DNA testing in suspected wrongful convictions. It also required preservation of biological evidence, which may hold key DNA, and improved legal services to those charged with capital crimes at both the state and federal levels. The Justice for All Act provided funds for improvements at state and local crime laboratories, including for training and DNA testing.

The law suggested (but did not require) compensation guidelines for those wrongfully convicted of crimes they did not commit. It suggested payment up to $50,000 for each year of wrongful incarceration except in death penalty cases. In those instances, the law suggested compensation of up to $100,000 for every year the person sat on death row. The guidelines only cover exonerated federal crimes. The act recommended, however, that states compensate those who are wrongfully convicted at the state level, particularly when they receive the death penalty as punishment. However, no minimum payments were established, and state courts are free to do as they choose.

As of 2014, more than half the states in the United States have laws that require some compensation for those exonerated.

For various reasons, only about two-thirds of exonerees get damage payments after being cleared of charges. For example, some states put restrictions on who can be compensated. Some states do not allow payments to anyone who contributed to his or her own conviction, whether through a false confession or through a plea bargain. Of those who are compensated, most wait an average of three to four years after exoneration before receiving any funds. This can be a real hardship. Exonerated men and women—like most people who have served time behind bars—typically leave prison with no money. They have few personal possessions, no means of transportation, no employment, and sometimes nowhere to stay.

In addition, almost all states make payments by annual installments only. This requires an exoneree—who has not been used to handling finances while in prison—to carefully manage the funds. If the exonerated person dies, the compensation is typically terminated. Funds often cannot be passed to heirs, even though they too suffered while a loved one was incarcerated. One expert points out that these policies have the most negative impact on elderly or sick prisoners. The policies are also more unfair to those whom the prosecution fights to keep in prison. In the end, the longer an innocent person remains incarcerated, the less likely that person is to be fully compensated, even if an award is made.

MOVING FORWARD TOGETHER

Even if those freed do receive a timely financial settlement, it never rights the wrongs a falsely convicted person has suffered. For this reason, a variety of organizations in the United States help exonerees reintegrate into society. Resurrection After Exoneration, in New Orleans, Louisiana, is one such organization. It is led by people who have themselves been exonerated. The agency assists individuals with a place to stay, job training, health care, mental health counseling, and guidance services. Some staff members of another group, Witness to Innocence, based in Philadelphia, Pennsylvania, were once on death row and have since been exonerated. The group works to educate the public and to abolish the death penalty in the United States. It also aids people convicted of capital crimes they didn't commit.

Exoneration groups are also working for change. David Moran, codirector of the Michigan Innocence Clinic (MIC), states, "Our plan is gradually to do more and more work to advocate for reform. Part of the idea of an innocence clinic is that we don't exonerate people quietly, and so a big part of our mission is to publicize these cases and explain what went wrong, and then use them as tools to try and convince policy makers and the public that these same mistakes shouldn't be made in the future." In Michigan, for example, the state bar association (a network representing attorneys practicing in the state) has created task forces to examine some of the issues that com-

> "A BIG PART OF OUR MISSION IS TO PUBLICIZE THESE CASES AND...CONVINCE POLICY MAKERS AND THE PUBLIC THAT THESE SAME MISTAKES SHOULDN'T BE MADE IN THE FUTURE."
> —David Moran, codirector of the Michigan Innocence Clinic, 2011

monly lead to wrongful convictions and to suggest remedies. One of the pilot research projects demonstrated that video recording of police interrogations helps avoid false convictions. In fact, the procedure actually improves the rate of proper convictions. Such findings will hopefully build support for other reforms and lead to new laws to help prevent future wrongful convictions.

The general public pays a big price for wrongful convictions. In Michigan, for example, the incarceration of each innocent person costs the state about $30,000 per year. People in prison are also not able to support their families financially. So, their families may have to seek welfare and other support payments from the government. After exoneration, financial compensation to the victims of unjust guilty verdicts costs taxpayers millions of dollars each year.

The greatest costs to society are not measured in dollars, however. When the actual perpetrators of serious and violent offenses get away with their crimes, they are free to commit additional unlawful acts. For example, evidence in four of the first five exonerations obtained by the MIC identified the real perpetrators. Those guilty individuals were alleged to have committed at least an additional six murders, a carjacking, and other offenses that could likely have been prevented. All those crimes took place after police mistakenly focused on innocent people as responsible for the real perpetrators' initial crimes. The general public also pays for false convictions by the damage they do to our trust in the legal system, which is fundamental to society.

SCIENCE AND JUSTICE: DOING THE RIGHT THING

The sciences of psychology, criminology, police science, and forensics work hand in hand with the legal system to prosecute and punish people whose actions break the laws that bind us into a community. One of the primary foundations of science is questioning. Good science, like justice, requires a willingness to keep an open mind and to consider all alternative possibilities when seeking truth. The mission of those involved in the science and service of justice is to never lose sight of the uncertainty that underlies all human endeavors, including their own. Criminal investigation and prosecution processes are complex and rely on people, who are all capable of mistakes. When errors are made, we must be open to correcting them.

The US Constitution establishes many rights. Along with these rights, Americans bear responsibilities to the government and to each other. As a society, each of us must strive to do our best and to attempt to be an ethical person of great character. All of us must aim to avoid situations where our integrity could be compromised. If we find ourselves in a moral dilemma, we must be strong in our convictions to do the right thing. We are called upon to respect authority. If we find ourselves as part of that authority—as a police officer, forensic scientist, judge, lawyer, or member of a jury—we must always aim to be worthy of that respect. Like the Innocence Project, the Center on Wrongful Convictions, and the Michigan Innocence Clinic, when we witness abuses of the legal system or people being treated unfairly, we too must work for change.

EXONERATED: DESHAWN AND MARVIN REED

In March 2000, twenty-two-year-old Shannon Gholston was driving in Ecorse, Michigan, just south of Detroit. He was turning left at an intersection when a bullet came through the window behind the driver's seat. The bullet hit him in the back of the neck and instantly paralyzed him. His car crashed into a fence, and when someone stopped to help and asked who had shot him, Gholston said

DeShawn Reed (left) and his uncle Marvin Reed (right) were imprisoned in 2001 for a drive-by shooting they did not commit. They were released in 2009 but struggled to get their lives back on track. In 2012 the city that investigated the men awarded the pair a $3.1 million settlement.

he didn't know. By the time he arrived at the hospital, he could barely whisper. A police officer shared with Gholston that people in the neighborhood were saying that either Gholston's former classmate, twenty-four-year-old DeShawn Reed, or his thirty-three-year-old uncle, Marvin Reed, was the shooter. The officer told Gholston to blink twice if DeShawn was the gunman. Gholston blinked twice. The officer asked the victim to blink twice if Marvin Reed was also involved in the shooting. Gholston again blinked two times.

Within the next few days, DeShawn and Marvin Reed were arrested and charged with assault with intent to commit murder. Both insisted they were innocent. A few weeks later, Gholston whispered sworn testimony from his hospital bed. He reported that Marvin was driving, with DeShawn as his passenger, when they pulled up alongside Gholston's car. Gholston reported that DeShawn (who is left handed) fired the shot from a gun in his right hand. When that testimony was presented at a preliminary hearing in 2000, a judge ordered the Reeds to stand trial the next year. DeShawn

and Marvin believed the truth would win out in time, once they got their day in court.

No physical evidence linked the Reeds to the crime, and the men had six alibi witnesses. Several eyewitnesses claimed they saw a man fire a couple shots from an alleyway behind Gholston's car, contradicting the victim's story. In fact, at least one witness had earlier told police the shooter was Tyrone Allen, who lived in the neighborhood and was involved with Gholston in a stolen car parts ring. Much of that information, however, never made it to trial. Allen himself couldn't be questioned. Police had shot and killed him during an attempted carjacking in the months just after Gholston was wounded.

It was clear the Reeds had had poor defense attorneys at trial. The judge himself stated that the complete story had likely not come out in court. All the same, he convicted both men of the murder and sentenced each to a minimum of twenty years in prison. Eight days after the Reeds were sentenced, the results of forensic bullet testing were released. Analysis showed that the bullet taken from Gholston's body at surgery matched the striation pattern on a bullet test-fired from a gun found on Allen after he had been shot by police.

The post-conviction bullet testing was new evidence that could not be used in the standard appeals process. Appeals were denied all the way up to the Michigan Supreme Court in 2005. DeShawn's younger brother then hired a private investigator. The investigator ultimately got Shannon Gholston to admit on videotape that he had not actually seen the person who shot him. Gholston claimed that once he had accused the Reeds and been backed by his entire family, he couldn't bring himself to say he had lied all along.

In 2007 a Reed family friend took the story to Northwestern University's Center on Wrongful Convictions. From there the case was passed to lawyer Bridget McCormack, who was forming the Michigan Innocence Clinic for non-DNA cases. She and another attorney prepared a motion requesting that the appellate court consider additional evidence. They found that the original police account of Gholston's eye-blink testimony in the hospital had been wrong. The officer had actually told him to blink twice if he did not know who had shot him, not if he did know. The MIC team also scientifically demonstrated that a bullet from a shooter in the alley in which Allen was supposedly standing could have easily penetrated Gholston's rear window on the driver's side, hitting the back of his neck as the car turned left. The alleged scenario—in which the shooter's car pulled up alongside Gholston so that the victim would have seen the shooter—was actually impossible.

The appeals court also reviewed evidence that before the Reeds' 2001 trial, Allen's girlfriend had told her uncle (a deputy sheriff) that Allen confessed to her that he had shot Gholston. The deputy notified the Ecorse police, but they apparently did not follow up on that claim.

The appeals court judge considered that information and ruled for a new trial. Before the trial took place, the charges were dropped in July 2009.

Third-year law student Zoe Levine (under the supervision of faculty members) represented the Reeds during the appeals process. She said of the experience, "I think when you're in that courtroom it's impossible not to feel . . . the stakes. You try your best to . . . make sure you do everything that you need to do for these clients because their lives are in the balance. They're also sitting there at the table with you . . . and behind you is their family and everyone is highly invested in this case, and so the pressure is very strong. The way to overcome that is preparation."

THE GIFT OF HOPE

DeShawn Reed said the exoneration team brought him the gift of hope. As a prisoner, he had not seen his four children grow up. The career goals he had been working toward when arrested were a thing of the past. DeShawn felt particularly bad, believing he was to blame for the conviction of his uncle Marvin and for all the years both men had spent in prison.

During the first four years of confinement, each man had spent twenty-three hours a day in his cell. Every time they were transferred to a new prison, they were strip-searched. Their cellmates were murderers, rapists, and other violent men. Once, in a case of mistaken identity, another prisoner stabbed DeShawn in the arm with a homemade knife. Marvin was put in solitary confinement for two days after a prison fight. Each man wondered whether having to defend himself against a fellow inmate might forever destroy his chances for a new trial.

The Reeds were finally set free in 2009. But they walked into a world that had changed both personally and technologically. Not wanting to wait twenty years for his release, the mother of DeShawn's children had moved on. Marvin had been newly married before his conviction, but his wife had divorced him while he was incarcerated. The two men left prison without a dime during one of the worst recessions the US economy has ever seen. They quickly discovered that convicts who are paroled after rightfully serving their time receive more help starting over than those who are wrongfully convicted.

DeShawn and Marvin Reed were each scheduled to receive $500 from the Ken Wyniemko Foundation. Wyniemko had started the fund after his own 2003 exoneration following a false conviction. DeShawn looked into getting his GED. He found that it was difficult to find work. Potential employers "want to know why you haven't been working for the last nine years. I still end up explaining the whole thing," he said. Complicating the men's ability to find work, their names remained in Michigan's online offender-tracking system until 2012 as part of state policy. Marvin took on odd jobs for a family member, saying, "I'm just trying to do an honest day's work."

In 2010 the MIC helped the Reeds file a wrongful conviction suit against the Ecorse Police Department. The men were awarded $3.1 million in 2012. Their story is one in which a close-knit neighborhood and three families were torn apart by a series of senseless acts. Shannon Gholston is a quadriplegic, Tyrone Allen is dead, and DeShawn and Marvin Reed spent years in prison for crimes they did not commit. The Reeds try never to be bitter about the time they spent behind bars and have forgiven Gholston.

EXONERATION PROFILES

The exoneration stories in this book are only a handful of the thousands of wrongful conviction stories in the United States. Below are brief sketches of a sampling of additional cases. To learn more about other exoneration stories, visit the National Registry of Exonerations website at https://www.law.umich.edu/special/exoneration/Pages/about.aspx Most cases have multiple causes for wrongful conviction.

Julie Baumer. In a 2003 Michigan case, twenty-seven-year-old Baumer was caring for her six-week-old nephew when he became ill. Hospital doctors suspected head trauma, perhaps from shaken baby syndrome. Baumer was charged with child abuse. Medical testimony disagreed on the injury's timing and cause, but Baumer was convicted and sentenced to ten to fifteen years. The appeals process resulted in a new trial at which six medical experts testified the baby had suffered a childhood stroke following a difficult delivery. Baumer was acquitted and exonerated in 2010.

Levon Brooks and Kennedy Brewer. A three-year-old girl was abducted, raped, and murdered in Mississippi in 1990. A forensic dentist named Dr. Michael West matched Levon Brooks (an ex-boyfriend of the child's mother) to the crime through bite-mark analysis. Brooks was convicted. A similar crime against another three-year-old was committed in the same town. Kennedy Brewer (the boyfriend of that child's mother) was convicted of that crime using bite-mark testimony from the same dentist. DNA testing exonerated both men in 2008 and uncovered the true perpetrator, who confessed. He said he had never bitten either girl, further calling into question the reliability of the forensic dentist, who was later discredited in numerous cases.

Francisco Carrillo. In a California case, police picked up Carrillo when he was fifteen for killing a man in front of the man's son and five other boys during a drive-by shooting. One witness claimed to have seen the gunman and told the others it was Carrillo. All six witnesses testified against Carrillo at trial, which ended in a hung jury. At his second trial, in 1992, Carrillo was convicted and sentenced to life in prison. While reviewing his own conviction case files in 2003, Carrillo discovered that a defense investigator had uncovered the real shooter. The shooter had confessed, but the judge had not permitted that testimony. The eyewitnesses eventually recanted and Carrillo was finally exonerated in 2011.

Rubin "Hurricane" Carter and John Artis. While preparing for the world middleweight boxing title in 1966, Carter and a friend, John Artis, were arrested for killing three people and wounding another in a New Jersey barroom shooting. After the grand jury failed to indict the men, police produced two informants. (They received reduced prison sentences and payments for their testimony.) Carter and Artis were sentenced to three life terms each. The informants recanted in 1974 and the convictions were overturned. However, the prosecution retried the men and they were again found guilty in 1976. Carter and Artis's convictions were finally reversed in 1985. Carter, who died in 2014, became one of the pioneers of and champions for exoneration.

Rolando Cruz and Alejandro Hernandez. Trying to gain a $10,000 reward for information related to the 1983 kidnapping, rape, and murder of a ten-year-old girl in Illinois, Rolando Cruz concocted a fake story. The plan backfired, and twenty-year-old Cruz, along with fellow gang member Alejandro Hernandez, age nineteen, were instead charged with the crime. The lead detective resigned in protest. Prosecutors tried the men anyway. They were sentenced to death, partly based on informant testimony. A serial killer named Brian Dugan had already confessed to the girl's murder, but that information was not presented at trial. An appeals court reversed the convictions based on legal errors, and the men were retried--this time as Dugan's accomplices. Both were again convicted. An assistant attorney general resigned, refusing to fight against further appeals, which were granted. The men endured a third trial before police corruption was revealed and DNA testing proved that the serial killer alone had been responsible. Cruz and Hernandez were freed after twelve years in prison.

William Dillon. In a 1981 Florida case, when he was twenty-one, Dillon was arrested for murder days before he was to try out for major league baseball. Five days after the murder, police picked up Dillon on the beach where the killing had occurred. Dillon admitted he knew about the case; it had been heavily covered in the news. A scent-tracking dog allegedly linked Dillon to bloody evidence, and he was arrested and later convicted, partly based on perjured testimony from his ex-girlfriend, who became romantically involved with the lead detective during the investigation. After Dillon had served almost twenty-seven years in prison, DNA evidence helped clear him in 2008.

Gary Dotson. In 1977 a sixteen-year-old Illinois girl told police she had been raped. The police collected her torn clothing and found a semen stain. After the girl described her attacker, police directed her to a photo of Dotson, who resembled the girl's description. Dotson was convicted in 1979. In 1985 the "victim" admitted she had made up the story. She had torn her own clothing, fearful of becoming pregnant after consensual sex with her boyfriend. The woman's attorney contacted the prosecutor's office that had convicted Dotson, but the office refused to investigate. In 1987 an attorney took on Dotson's case after learning about the confirmation that new DNA testing could provide. Dotson was finally exonerated in 1989.

Dennis Fritz and Ronald Williamson. In an Oklahoma case, Fritz (age twenty-two) and Williamson (age twenty-nine) were both convicted in 1988 for raping and killing a young woman whose body had been found six years earlier. A day before charges against Fritz were to be dropped for insufficient evidence, Fritz's cellmate alleged that Fritz had confessed to him. Another witness perjured herself against Williamson, who later came within five days of execution. Both men were exonerated in 1999 after DNA testing showed that one of the prosecution's witnesses who had testified against Williamson was the actual rapist. The book *The Innocent Man: Murder and Injustice in a Small Town* by John Grisham covers this case.

Barry Gibbs. In New York, a witness claimed to have seen a man wearing red pants dump a woman's body from a gray car. Detective Louis Eppolito heard that Gibbs knew the victim and brought him in for a lineup. The witness identified Gibbs. A jailhouse informant testified Gibbs had confessed to him while awaiting trial. Evidence included a pair of red pants police allegedly discovered in Gibbs's apartment, although they didn't fit him. Gibbs also had a gray car, but it was inoperable and had flat tires. Gibbs was convicted of murder in 1988. The police file in Gibbs's case and DNA evidence went missing, complicating appeals. In 2005 police began investigating Eppolito, who had retired, and found Gibbs's missing file in his home. Later, he and another officer were convicted for eight murders and other crimes they had committed for the Mafia. The witness against Gibbs admitted that Eppolito had threatened him and his family if he did not help frame Gibbs. After spending more than seventeen years in prison, Gibbs was exonerated in 2005.

Calvin C. Johnson Jr. Two women, both raped in Georgia in 1983, ultimately identified twenty-five-year-old Johnson as their attacker. One woman picked him from among a group of photos. However, she could not identify him later in a police lineup. The second woman did not choose Johnson from a photo array but did select him during a lineup. Despite the conflicting eyewitness identifications, Johnson was convicted in one of the rape trials and was acquitted in the other. Johnson served sixteen years of a life sentence, and in 1997, DNA testing showed that he was not the rapist. In 1999 a judge ordered a new trial, but based on the DNA results, the district attorney dropped charges. Johnson's case is the subject of the 2005 book *Exit to Freedom*.

Koua Fong Lee. After ramming his Toyota into another car and killing three people in Minnesota, Lee was sentenced to eight years in prison for vehicular homicide in 2007. Lee claimed the car had accelerated on its own, and he had tried to stop. Lee's defense lawyer told the jury his client may have hit the gas pedal while intending to hit the brake, since there was no evidence of skid marks at the scene. Lee's appeal attorney indicated the antilock breaking system on his car would not have caused skid marks even if he had tried to stop. Based on the initial lawyer's negligence, Lee won a new trial. He was released in 2010, as evidence of problems with vehicle acceleration mounted.

Jerry Miller. In 1981 an Illinois woman who routinely used the same parking garage was shoved into her car, beaten, robbed, raped, and then forced into her trunk. When the perpetrator tried to drive out of the garage, the gate attendant recognized the victim's car and confronted the driver, who ran off. Two parking employees helped generate a police sketch. Police arrested twenty-three-year-old Miller. He resembled the sketch, and both garage attendants picked him out of a lineup. The victim was unable to identify Miller from photos. However, at trial she claimed he resembled her attacker. DNA testing finally exonerated Miller in 2007. He had already been released by this time, however.

SOURCE NOTES

4 William Blackstone, *Commentaries on the Laws of England,* 4 vols, (Oxford: Clarendon Press, 1765-1769), bk. 4, ch. 27. Available at http://library.law.harvard.edu/justicequotes/explore-the-room/south-4/.

7 Ken Burns, Sarah Burns, and David McMahon, *The Central Park Five,* directed by Ken Burns, Sarah Burns, and David McMahon (New York: IFC Films/Sundance Selects, 2012), DVD.

8 Alice Cantwell, "Sentencing in Central Park Attack," *New York Daily News,* January 10, 1991, accessed May 27, 2014, http://www.nydailynews.com/services/central-park-five/sentencing-central-park-attack-article-1.1304989.

8 Sarah Burns, *Central Park Five: A Chronicle of a City Wilding.* (New York: Knopf, 2011), 150.

8 Lizzette Alverez, "Central Park Attackers Sentenced to Max," *New York Daily News,* September 12, 1990, accessed May 27, 2014, http://www.nydailynews.com/services/central-park-five/central-park-attackers-sentenced-max-article-1.1304884.

9 Burns, Burns, and McMahon. *The Central Park Five* (DVD).

9 Ibid.

9 Ibid.

10 Benjamin Weiser, "5 Exonerated in Central Park Jogger Case Agree to Settle Suit for $40 Million," *New York Times,* June 19, 2014, accessed June 22, 2014, http://www.nytimes.com/2014/06/20/nyregion/5-exonerated-in-central-park-jogger-case-are-to-settle-suit-for-40-million.html?smid=fb-share&_r=2.

12 Calvin C. Johnson Jr., and Greg Hampikian (with an afterword by Barry Scheck), *Exit to Freedom: The Only Firsthand Account of a Wrongful Conviction Overturned by DNA Evidence.* (Athens, GA: University of Georgia Press, 2003), 271.

24 Innocence Project, "DNA Exoneree Case Profiles," accessed April 11, 2014, http://www.innocenceproject.org/know/.

36 John Grisham, *Innocence Project: John Grisham Discusses "The Innocent Man,"* clip from Innocence Project annual benefit video, 2008, http://www.innocenceproject.org/news/Video/?id=tpEQfagdfXk.

48 Decca Aitkenhead, "Betty Ann Waters: 'We Thought Kenny Was Coming

Home',” *Guardian,* December 10, 2010, accessed June 16, 2013, http://www.theguardian.com/film/2010/dec/11/betty-anne-waters-interview.

48 Ibid.

50 Jennifer Thompson-Cannino, Ronald Cotton, and Erin Torneo, *Picking Cotton: Our Memoir of Injustice and Redemption* (New York: St. Martin's Press, 2009), 68.

57 Ibid., 172.

57 Ibid., 271–272.

58 Christopher Ochoa, “My Life Is a Broken Puzzle” in *Surviving Justice: America's Wrongfully Convicted and Exonerated,* compiled and edited by Dave Eggers and Lola Vollen (San Francisco: McSweeney's Publishing, 2005), 19.

65 Lisa Chavarria, “Chicago Mom Freed after Serving Seven Years on Wrongful Conviction,” *myFOXChicago.com,* June 24, 2013, accessed April 30, 2014, http://www.myfoxchicago.com/story/22614447/chicago-mom-freed-from-prison-after-7-years-on-wrongful-conviction#ixzz2WaGPYcPz%3Cbr%20/%3E.

65 Ibid.

66 Innocence Project, “National Academy of Sciences Urges Comprehensive Reform of U.S. Forensic Sciences,” February 18, 2009, accessed June 12, 2014, http://www.innocenceproject.org/Content/National_Academy_of_Sciences_Urges_Comprehensive_Reform_of_US_Forensic_Sciences.php.

73 Francis X. Clines, “Work by Expert Witness Is Now on Trial,” *New York Times,* September 5, 2001, accessed June 16, 2013, http://www.nytimes.com/2001/09/05/us/work-by-expert-witness-is-now-on-trial.html.

74 Rob Warden, *The Snitch System: How Snitch Testimony Sent Randy Steidl and Other Innocent Americans to Death Row* (Chicago: Center on Wrongful Convictions, 2004), 2. Available at http://www.innocenceproject.org/docs/SnitchSystemBooklet.pdf.

77 Ibid., 15.

78 Alexis Wiley, “New Evidence Could Lead to Convicted Detroit Man's Exoneration,” clip from *myFOXDetroit.com,* November 20, 2012, accessed June 15, 2014, http://www.myfoxdetroit.com/story/20144768/new-evidence-could-lead-to-convicted-murderers-exoneration.

79 Alexis Wiley, "Local Man Wrongly Convicted of Murder to Be Set Free," clip from *myFOX9.com,* December 13, 2013, accessed June 15, 2014, http://www.myfoxtwincities.com/story/24219389/local-man-wrongly-convicted-of-murder-to-be-set-free.

80 Peter Rose, "People Don't Know How Lucky They Are to Have Their Liberty" in *Surviving Justice: America's Wrongfully Convicted and Exonerated,* compiled and edited by Dave Eggers and Lola Vollen (San Francisco: McSweeney's Publishing, 2005), 439.

87 Brooke A. Masters, "Missteps on the Road to Injustice: How Earl Washington, Jr. Was Sent to Death Row for a Crime He Did Not Commit," *Washington Post,* November 30, 2000, accessed May 27, 2014. Available at http://truthinjustice.org/missteps.htm.

90 National Registry of Exonerations, *Exonerations in 2013,* February 4, 2014, https://www.law.umich.edu/special/exoneration/Documents/Exonerations_in_2013_Report.pdf, 4.

96 Christina Schockley, Zoe Clark, and What's Working, "Michigan Innocence Clinic Works to Free Those Wrongfully Convicted," *Michigan Radio,* June 24, 2011, accessed June 22, 2014, http://michiganradio.org/post/michigan-innocence-clinic-works-free-those-wrongfully-convicted.

102 "Out of the Blue: The Michigan Difference: Innocence Clinic," *University of Michigan,* Michigan Television Production, n.d., accessed June 16, 2013, http://web.law.umich.edu/flashmedia/public/Default.aspx?mediaid=133.

103 James Dickson, "After Eight Years of Wrongful Imprisonment, the Reeds Are Free with the Help of University of Michigan's Innocence Clinic. But Now What?" *Ann Arbor News,* September 17, 2009. http://www.annarbor.com/news/exonerated-but-now-what/.

103 Ibid.

SELECTED BIBLIOGRAPHY

Acker, James R., and Allison D. Redlich. *Wrongful Conviction: Law, Science, and Policy.* Durham, NC: Carolina Academic Press, 2011.

Bohm, Robert M. *Capital Punishment's Collateral Damage.* Durham, NC: Carolina Academic Press, 2012.

Committee on Commerce, Science, and Transportation, United States Senate, Hearing before the One Hundred Twelfth Congress, First Session, December 7, 2011. *Turning the Investigation on the Science of Forensics.* Washington, DC: US Government Printing Office, 2013. Available at http://www.gpo.gov/fdsys/pkg/CHRG-112shrg77805/pdf/CHRG-112shrg77805.pdf.

Committee on Identifying the Needs of the Forensic Sciences Community, National Research Council. *Strengthening Forensic Science in the United States: A Path Forward.* Washington, DC: US Department of Justice, 2009. Available at https://www.ncjrs.gov/pdffiles1/nij/grants/228091.pdf.

Garrett, Brandon L. *Convicting the Innocent: Where Criminal Prosecutions Go Wrong.* Cambridge: Harvard University Press, 2012.

Harris, David A. *Failed Evidence: Why Law Enforcement Resists Science.* New York: New York University Press, 2012.

Lassiter, G. Daniel, and Christian A. Meissner. *Police Interrogations and False Confessions: Current Research, Practice, and Policy Recommendations.* Washington DC: American Psychological Association, 2010.

Medwed, Daniel S. *Prosecution Complex: America's Race to Convict and Its Impact on the Innocent.* New York: New York University Press, 2012.

Petro, Jim, and Nancy Petro. *False Justice: Eight Myths That Convict the Innocent.* New York: Kaplan Publishing, 2011.

Simon, Dan. *In Doubt: The Psychology of the Criminal Justice Process.* Cambridge: Harvard University Press, 2012.

Walker, Jeffrey R., and Craig Hemmens. *Legal Guide for Police: Constitutional Issues,* 9th ed. Cincinnati: Anderson Publishing, 2010.

Zalman, Marvin, and Julia Carrano. *Wrongful Conviction and Criminal Justice Reform: Making Justice* (Criminology and Justice Studies). London: Routledge, 2013.

FOR FURTHER INFORMATION

Borchard, Edwin M. *Convicting the Innocent: Sixty Five Actual Errors of Criminal Justice.* Scotts Valley, CA: CreateSpace, 2010 (republication of Garden City, NY: Yale University Press edition, 1932).
The 1932 edition is available in its entirety at https://archive.org/details/convictinginnoce00borchrich.

Burns, Ken, Sarah Burns, and David McMahon. *The Central Park Five.* Directed by Ken Burns, Sarah Burns, and David McMahon. New York: IFC Films/Sundance Selects, 2012. DVD.
This documentary covers the story of five teens, Antron McCray, Kevin Richardson, Yusef Salaam, Raymond Santana, and Korey Wise, who were wrongfully convicted in 1990 for rape and were exonerated in 2002.

Burns, Sarah. *The Central Park Five: A Chronicle of Wilding.* New York: Knopf, 2011.

Center on Wrongful Convictions, Bluhm Legal Clinic, Northwestern University School of Law. http://www.law.northwestern.edu/legalclinic/wrongfulconvictions/
This website provides information about wrongful convictions and related issues, includes a list of exonerated, and features videos, news segments, and a blog.

Connors, Edward, Thomas Lundregan, Neal Miller, and Tom McEwen. *Convicted by Juries, Exonerated by Science: Case Studies in the Use of DNA Evidence to Establish Innocence after Trial.* US Department of Justice, Office of Justice Programs, National Institute of Justice, 1996. PDF.
These studies are available by cutting and pasting the following URL into your browser: http://permanent.access.gpo.gov/lps53435/lps53435.pdf.

Edds, Margaret. *An Expendable Man: The Near Execution of Earl Washington Jr.* New York: New York University Press, 2003.

Eggers, David, and Lola Vollen, eds. *Surviving Justice: America's Wrongfully Convicted and Exonerated.* San Francisco: McSweeney's Publishing, 2005.

Fritz, Dennis. *Journey toward Justice.* Santa Ana, CA: Seven Locks Press, 2006.

Gray, Pamela. *Conviction.* Directed by Tony Goldwyn. Los Angeles: Fox Searchlight Pictures, 2010. DVD.
This film tells the true story of Kenny Waters, who was wrongfully convicted of murder in 1983. His sister Betty Anne Waters became an attorney and helped to exonerate him. He was freed in 2001.

Grisham, John. *The Innocent Man: Murder and Injustice in a Small Town.* New York: Doubleday, 2012.

Innocence Project. http://www.innocenceproject.org/
This is the official website of the Innocence Project, affiliated with the Benjamin N. Cardozo School of Law at Yeshiva University in New York. The site provides case profiles of its exonerees and information about the causes of wrongful convictions, including video segments to highlight facts and figures.

Johnson Jr., Calvin C., and Greg Hampikian (with an afterword by Barry Scheck). *Exit to Freedom.* Athens: University of Georgia Press, 2005.

Junkin, Tim. *Bloodsworth: The True Story of One Man's Triumph over Injustice.* Chapel Hill, NC: Algonquin Books, 2005.

Loftus, Elizabeth F. *Eyewitness Testimony.* Cambridge, MA: Harvard University Press, 1996.

Loftus, Elizabeth, and Katherine Ketcham. *Witness for the Defense: The Accused, the Eyewitness, and the Expert Who Puts Memory on Trial.* New York: St. Martin's Press, 1991.

Meili, Trisha. *I Am the Central Park Jogger: A Story of Hope and Possibility.* New York: Scribner, 2003.

Michigan Innocence Clinic at Michigan Law
https://www.law.umich.edu/clinical/innocenceclinic/Pages/default. aspx This is the website of the Michigan Innocence Clinic, where information about the causes of wrongful convictions and case summaries (for non-DNA exonerations) can be found, as well as a 2009 video (on the "In the News" page) about the exoneration of DeShawn and Marvin Reed, the clinic's first two clients.

Münsterberg, Hugo. *On the Witness Stand: Essays on Psychology and Crime,* (n.p., 1908, revised in 1925).

114

These essays are available at no cost from Classics in Psychology at http://psychclassics.yorku.ca/Munster/Witness/index.htm

National Registry of Exonerations
http://www.law.umich.edu/special/exoneration/Pages/about.aspx
The registry lists all known exonerations since 1989 and includes exoneree case information and other resources to help site visitors better understand wrongful convictions.

Center on Wrongful Convictions, Bluhm Legal Clinic, Northwestern University School of Law
http://www.law.northwestern.edu/legalclinic/wrongfulconvictions/
This website provides information about wrongful convictions and related issues, includes a list of exonerated people, and features videos, news segments, and a blog.

Scheck, Barry, Peter Neufeld, and Jim Dwyer. *Actual Innocence: When Justice Goes Wrong and How to Make It Right.* New York: Signet, 2001.

Shelton, Donald E. *Forensic Science in Court: Challenges in the Twenty-First Century* (Issues in Crime and Justice). Lanham, MD: Rowman & Littlefield, 2011.

Thompson-Cannino, Jennifer, and Ronald Cotton, with Erin Torneo. *Picking Cotton: Our Memoir of Injustice and Redemption.* New York: St. Martin's Press, 2009.

Warden, Rob. *The Snitch System: How Snitch Testimony Sent Randy Steidl and Other Innocent Americans to Death Row.* Chicago: Center on Wrongful Convictions, 2004. Available at http://www.innocenceproject.org/docs/SnitchSystemBooklet.pdf.

Warden, Rob, and Steven A. Drizin. *True Stories of False Confessions.* Chicago: Northwestern University Press, 2009.

Wells, Tom, and Richard A. Leo. *The Wrong Guys: Murder, False Confessions, and the Norfolk Four.* New York: New Press, 2008.

Westervelt, Saundra D., and Kimberly J. Cook. *Life after Death Row: Exonerees' Search for Community and Identity* (Critical Issues in Crime and Society). New Brunswick, NJ: Rutgers University Press, 2012.

INDEX

PHOTO ACKNOWLEDGMENTS

The images in this book are used with the permission of: © iStockphoto.com/fpm (prison bars); © iStockphoto.com/VallarieE (rusty barbed wire); © iStockphoto.com/Trevor Hunt (newspaper tear); © fhogue/Thinkstock, p. 4; © Michael Nagle/The New York Times/Redux, p. 10; © iStockphoto.com/WSS, p. 12; AP Photo, p. 16; © iStockphoto.com/Terraxplorer, p. 24; Courtesy of The Innocence Project, p. 27; © Laura Westlund/Independent Picture Service, pp. 30, 92; © iStockphoto.com/dvan, p. 36; AP Photo/Steven Senne, p. 47; © iStockphoto.com/redhumv, p. 50; AP Photo/The News & Observer/Takaaki Iwabu, p. 55; © Ivan Bliznetsov/Getty Images, p. 58; © Zbigniew Bzdak/Chicago Tribune/MCT/LANDOV , p. 63; © iStockphoto.com/dra_schwartz, p. 66; AP Photo/The Daily Oklahoman, Roger Klock, p. 68; © David Schalliol/Moment/Getty Images, p. 74; © Bryce Duffy/The Image Bank/Getty Images, p. 80; AP Photo/Steve Helber, p. 85; © motorenmano/E+/Getty Images, p. 90; © Lon Horwedel, p. 99.

Front cover: © iStockphoto.com/GlobalP (crow); © iStockphoto.com/fpm (prison bars); © iStockphoto.com/VallarieE, (barbed wire).

LERNER

e

SOURCE

Expand learning beyond the printed book. Download free, complementary educational resources for this book from our website, www.lerneresource.com.

ABOUT THE AUTHOR

Dr. Elizabeth A. Murray has been an educator and a forensic scientist for more than twenty-five years. Her primary teaching focus is human anatomy and physiology and forensic science. She is one of only about seventy anthropologists certified as an expert by the American Board of Forensic Anthropology. Dr. Murray was scientific consultant and on-camera personality for the miniseries *Skeleton Crew* for the National Geographic Channel and a regular cast member on the Discovery Health Channel series *Skeleton Stories.* She has written and delivered two lecture series, *Trails of Evidence: How Forensic Science Works and Forensic History: Crimes, Frauds, and Scandals,* produced on DVD by The Teaching Company's The Great Courses. Dr. Murray is also the author of *Forensic Identification: Putting a Name and Face on Death* and *of Death: Corpses, Cadavers, and Other Grave Matters* for teen readers.

ACKNOWLEDGMENTS

Many thanks are due to my longstanding friends Chief Magistrate Michael L. Bachman and court reporter Linda Mallory, both from the Hamilton County, Ohio, Court of Common Pleas, for reviewing legal aspects of this work. Chief Deputy Mark Whittaker of Darke County, Ohio, once again assisted me with a deeper understanding of best police practices. My sister Kathy Isaacs and my dear friend Elizabeth Villing provided thoughtful comments on the first draft. Thanks to Domenica Di Piazza of Lerner Publishing Group for her patience and wise responses to my many questions. I want to express gratitude to my family for understanding all the times I was busy. Finally, I wish to recognize the exonerees whose public stories of battles won have allowed me to include them in this book. May your cases, and the too many others like yours, inspire all of us to consistently strive to prevent injustices, whenever and wherever we see them.